Discovering God Together

Dr. Gregory K. and Lisa Popcak

Discovering God Together

The Catholic Guide to Raising Faithful Kids

SOPHIA INSTITUTE PRESS
Manchester, New Hampshire

Sophia Institute Press
Box 5284, Manchester, NH 03108
1-800-888-9344

www.SophiaInstitute.com

Sophia Institute Press® is a registered trademark of Sophia Institute.

Library of Congress Cataloging-in-Publication Data

Popcak, Gregory K.
  Discovering God together: the Catholic guide to raising faithful kids / Dr. Gregory K. and Lisa Popcak.
      pages cm
  Includes bibliographical references.
  ISBN 978-1-62282-246-1 (pbk. : alk. paper) 1. Christian education of children. 2. Catholic Church—Doctrines. 3. Catholic Church—Education. 4. Child rearing—Religious aspects—Catholic Church. 5. Parenting—Religious aspects—Catholic Church. I. Title.
  BV1475.3.P67 2015
  248.8'45—dc23

                                                            2015018434

To our children:
may the light of God's grace
guide your paths and ignite your hearts
with the fire of his love

Contents

Part 3
Meet the Family:
Connecting Kids to the Community of Faith

Discovering God Together

Part 1

Your Faith Journey:
Getting the Lay of the Land

1

Discovering God Together: An Invitation

Raising a child — much more, a *faithful* child — is both an amazing blessing and a huge responsibility. All of us want to give our children the best. We wish them joy, peace, love, health, good values, and, of course, as Christians, we want them to have eternal life. But how do we share our faith in a way that will make sense to our kids and stick with them for a lifetime?

St. Paul tells of how we struggle to see God clearly (1 Cor. 13:12). Because of our own mixed experiences with life and spirituality, we often feel as if we're looking through a dirty window when it comes to trying to understand, much less explain, our faith. We might carry emotional and spiritual wounds that can further cloud or complicate our relationship with God. When we combine these issues with the simple challenges of getting through the day, it's not surprising that God often doesn't register on our personal radar. If he does, we might think of him in ways that make him seem remote or even suspicious.

Regardless of where you find yourself on the spiritual path, God is inviting you to deepen your relationship with him and to share that journey with your children to help them on their way to claiming every good and perfect gift that comes from him (see James 1:17).

Of course God wants your child to know his deep and abiding love, but he wants that for you too. Even more than you want to give every good thing to your child, God wants to give his love, his grace, and his healing to you (see Matt. 7:11).

There are many reasons — both spiritual and practical — that families benefit from cultivating their faith together. As you will discover in these pages, research shows again and again that when families openly live and share their faith, marriages become stronger, children and parents get along better, and children are less likely to succumb to drugs, alcohol, promiscuity, and negative peer pressure (Fagan, 2006). And those are only the temporal payoffs in this world! All the graces that we receive while pursuing a relationship of faith here also help secure sure and certain hope of everlasting life!

"Doing Faith" with Our Kids

Yet even with all this to motivate us, the idea of passing on our faith to our children can often seem intimidating. We are busy or feel too weak in our faith or feel that our faith is too private to share. No one ever really taught us how to "do faith" with kids. These and many more reasons can often lead even the most well-meaning parents to default to attempting to pass on the faith to children by checking off the right boxes:

Take child to church. *Check.*

Learn all the rote prayers. *Check.*

Send child to the right school. *Check.*

Set down the rules and regulations at home. *Check.*

Although each of these elements is an important part of passing on the faith, they often fall tremendously short of helping our children develop a true and lasting relationship with God. They can help form a whole picture of the faith for our children *only* when they are connected to the love that springs from God's heart, a love that ties us to him and to each member of our household.

In the following pages, you will explore many ways for you and your children to discover God *together* in the big and small moments of your everyday family life and learn how to tap into the rich beauty of the sacraments and traditions of our Catholic faith. The Bible encourages us to share faith with our children when we sit at home and when we walk along the road, when we go to bed and when we rise (see Deut. 11:19). As you read this book, it is our hope that you will find many new and exciting ways to encounter God in your home, in your community, and in your life, so that every moment with your children can be filled with God's grace, joy, love, and abundance.

Let the adventure begin!

2

What Makes Catholic Families Different?
The Five Marks of a Faithful Family

At the beginning of any journey, you need good directions, or a GPS, so you'll know where you're going. If you begin a trip planning to make your way up as you go, you might not ever arrive at your intended destination. Even if you have a set of old directions that used to be correct, who's to say that the route hasn't changed? You need the most current directions to help you get from A to B.

The same might be said for your spiritual journey with your kids. If you want to arrive at your destination—the point where your kids are ready to launch out into the world as faithful, Catholic young adults—you can't just wing it. And the directions your parents or grandparents used might not get you there. It's a different world with a completely new landscape and more roads than ever for you and your kids to get lost on. To get where you're going, you will have to begin your journey with a clear sense of the route ahead, and you will need to be more intentional than ever about making sure you stay on the right roads.

Finding the Address

To start, you have to ask yourself, "Is it enough for me to raise *basically* faithful kids?" In other words, do you want to help your kids arrive safely at the address marked "Faithful Catholic Adult-hood," or is any other address in the neighborhood (e.g., "Faith-ful Nondenominational Christian" or "Spiritual, Not Religious") just as good?

Assuming that you're more particular about helping your kids get to the address marked "Faithful Catholic Adulthood," you will have to give them an example of Catholic family life that's worth repeating in adulthood. This involves two things.

1. Parents have to give their kids a family life that they experience as truly better—not necessarily perfect, but more honest, intimate, generous, and joyful—than most of their non-Catholic friends' experience of family.

2. Your children have to know in their guts that it is your love for Jesus Christ and your Catholic faith that are responsible for that more honest, intimate, joyful, and generous experience of family life. Why is this so im-portant? As you will see, the research is clear: for most people, but especially for kids, faith development is all about relationship. If your kids don't experience their uniquely Catholic faith making a positive, tangible dif-ference in their everyday lives, their faith won't survive to adulthood—especially not in today's world with so many other lifestyles from which to choose.

Identifying the Catholic Difference

How are Catholic families supposed to be different from other families? We don't mean different in the sense of putting on airs, pretending to be holier than thou, or acting weird in some way. But if you read the Church's writings on marriage and fam-ily life, you'll see that the Church is on a mission to promote a particular vision of family life that is different from that of other families, in the sense that it is more intimate, more joyful, more "together."

In *The Gospel of Life*, St. John Paul the Great put forth what might be considered the mission statement for Catholic parents in contemporary times.

> By word and example, in the daily round of relations and choices, and through concrete actions and signs, parents lead their children to authentic freedom, actualized in the sincere gift of self, and they cultivate in them respect for others, a sense of justice, cordial openness, dialogue, generous service, solidarity and all the other values which help people to live life as a gift. (no. 92)

This is the unique, Catholic vision of family life Catholic parents are called to uphold. Clearly it is a different vision of family life from the one that the world has to offer.

Sadly, too many Catholic kids are being raised in homes that don't look any different from the homes of their secular or Protestant friends except for the prayers they say and maybe the rules they have. As a result, Catholic parents are undermining their own best efforts to raise faithful children and to bear witness to the joy of the gospel. As Christians, we are called to be salt and light in the world—God wants to change the world through the example of love lived out in our families—but how can we change the world if we look and act exactly like everyone else? In order for our faith to seem relevant to our children and to the world at large, Catholic couples and families must present a vision of love that shows our children that our Catholic faith can satisfy the longings of their heart, a vision of love that makes the world stand up and take notice.

Discovering God Together

Living the Mission: Five Marks of the Catholic Family

So how do we do it? How do we enable our kids to experience the practical, positive, tangible difference our faith should make in our family life? We suggest that the following five traits distinguish a family seeking to live the authentic Catholic difference in their daily lives.

1. *Catholic families worship together.* The Eucharist is the source of our love and the sign of the intimacy to which we are called. Therefore, as a family, we attend Mass together on Sundays and holy days (and at other times as we are able), and we actively participate in our parish.

We also recognize that, as fallen persons, we struggle to be the loving community we are called to be. Therefore, as a family, we regularly go to Confession (recommended: monthly) to seek God's healing and grace so we might better live his vision of love in our lives and homes.

Questions for Reflection

1. What would we need to do to get to Mass as a family more often?

2. How could we make going to Mass as a family a more intimate and relationship-building experience?

3. What could we do to get to Confession as a family at least once a month?

2. *Catholic families pray together.* The Church refers to the family as the "domestic church" because family life is where the faith is supposed to be lived out every day. Catholic families are called to love each other not only with their human love but also with the love that flows from God's heart. As Catholic families, we

recognize that we cannot love one another as God loves us unless we ask him — *together* — to teach us what this means. Therefore, in addition to our individual prayer life and our worship with our parish communities, we gather together both as husband and wife and also as a family for prayer each day.

In these times, we:

- praise and thank God for his blessings

- ask forgiveness for the times we did not love him and each other as we ought

- ask for the grace to love each other and the world better

- seek his will for our lives

- pray for our needs and the needs of the Family of God

We recognize in the words of Servant of God Fr. Patrick Peyton, "the family that prays together stays together."

Questions for Reflection

1. What could we do to make family prayer happen every day?

2. What could we do to make family prayer a more intimate and relationship-building experience?

3. *Catholic families are called to intimacy.* Tertullian once proclaimed, "The world says, 'Look at those Christians, see how they love one another!'" The Christian life is first and foremost a call to intimate communion. As St. Jean Vianney said, "Prayer is nothing less than union with God."[1]

---

[1] Quoted in Robert Atwell, ed., *Celebrating the Saints* (Norwich: Canterbury Press, 1998), 429.

We recognize that families are "schools of love" in which we learn how to love God and each other. Therefore, as a family, we constantly challenge ourselves to seek new ways to be more open with and loving toward each other as husband and wife, parents and children.

We recognize that children are to be a visible sign of the loving union between husband and wife, and we work to make this a reality in our homes, both in our openness to life and by working hard on the quality of our relationships with each other.

Further, we cultivate marriage and parenting practices that make all members of the family willing to open up to one another and to give themselves freely to create a deeper "community of love" and practice all the virtues.

Questions for Reflection

1. What do we see as obstacles to our sharing our thoughts, feelings, hopes, dreams, and needs with each other?

2. What do we need to do to overcome those obstacles to sharing our hearts more deeply as a family and becoming the "community of love" we are meant to be? What resources (books, courses) or assistance (classes, spiritual direction, or professional counseling) might we need to overcome those obstacles?

4. *Catholic families put family first.* We recognize that, because our family relationships are the primary vehicle God uses to perfect us and challenge us to become everything we were created to be, *family life itself is the most important activity in our week.* To protect the intimacy we are called to cultivate as the domestic church, we recognize the importance of regular family rituals, and we are intentional about creating and protecting those activities, such

as family dinners, family prayer and worship, game nights and "family days," and regular, scheduled time for one-on-one communication and relationship building. We hold these activities as sacred rituals of the domestic church and value them over all other activities that would seek to compete with them.

Questions for Reflection

1. What are the favorite activities we do to work, play, talk, and pray together as a family?

2. How could we make those activities happen more regularly as a family? What changes would we need to make to prioritize daily and weekly times to work, play, talk, and pray as a family?

5. *The Catholic family is a witness and a sign.* God wants to change the world through our families. We allow ourselves to be part of his plan for changing the world in two ways. First, we strive to exhibit — in every way possible in our daily interactions — the closeness, love, and intimacy for which every human heart longs.

Second, we carry this love outside the home by serving the world at large in a manner that is responsible and respectful of the integrity of our family relationships. We do this by committing ourselves and our families to the intentional practice of the Corporal and Spiritual Works of Mercy in the home and outside it. To this end, the ways in which we, as a family, try to fulfill this responsibility will be a regular topic of conversation in our homes.

Questions for Reflection

1. In our daily life, when do we feel closest as a family? What would we need to do to make these times happen more often?

2. How do we serve the Church and community as a family? Of the things we do to serve the Church or the community, what enables us to draw closer as a family?

This might be an incomplete list. Nevertheless, we believe it represents the kind of effort that we parents must undertake if we want to raise kids who have a faith that sticks with them as they enter into adulthood and seek to form their own families.

Don't Worry, Be Catholic

In reviewing this list, you might feel as if you fall a little short. Don't worry about it. No family is perfect. You don't have to be all of these things overnight, and this book is dedicated to helping you live up to the mission we've described in this chapter. But however you imagine your family compares with the mission we've laid out, we hope you will let this list be your roadmap.

Let these five marks of a Catholic family be the vision you look to as you make decisions about the activities your kids are involved in, the way you set your schedule, organize your priorities, make decisions, and plan your day. Keep these five points in mind as you explore even more ways for you and your children to discover God together as he draws you closer to him through the ups and downs and ins and outs of your everyday family life.

3

Life in the Domestic Church:
Rituals and Routines

Our life in our Catholic parish, our Church family, is filled with rituals. Our liturgical calendar is filled with feasts, fast days, holy days, and other celebrations. These rituals become the rhythm by which we live our life of faith. They help us to regulate the seasons of our spiritual life, making sure that all God's Family attends to each of the important aspects of our life of faith; celebration, repentance, reflection, and resolving to go deeper in our relationship with God.

Similarly, our Church-family life is filled with routines. When we gather to worship as the Family of God, things are done in a certain manner that enables our whole self—body, mind, and spirit—to focus on strengthening our connection with God and with all our brothers and sisters who are saying the same familiar prayers and singing the same familiar songs and participating in the same familiar gestures as we are. By participating in these rituals and routines, we foster a deep sense of belonging to our family of faith.

God strengthens the relationship of his family through rituals and routines. As common and familiar as they are, they contain incredible power. Our consistent participation in these rituals and routines becomes part of us and anchors us, both to God and to the community of faith.

Sacred Life in the Domestic Church

In the same way, life in the domestic church—our family life—is ordered by the rituals and routines we celebrate at home that help govern how and how often we work, play, talk, and pray together.

More than sixty years of research shows that, almost more than any other factor, the presence of regular rituals and routines that govern how and how often the family works, plays, talks, and prays together (e.g., family meals, game nights, prayer time, family days, holidays and celebrations, chores, bedtime routines, and so forth) dictates both how stable and how happy that family will be together over time (Fiese, 2006). Rituals and routines create order in family life as well as a sense of community. Families with well-defined rituals and routines have been shown to be physically and emotionally healthier, have better academic outcomes, and are more resistant to depression, anxiety, substance abuse, promiscuity, obesity, and a host of other personal, emotional, and relationship problems (Fiese, 2006). If it were possible to put into a pill all the benefits a person could gain by growing up in a family with strong rituals and routines that govern work, play, talk, and prayer, the person who accomplished such a feat would not only become wealthy overnight but would no doubt also win the Nobel Prize for medicine. Rituals and routines are as close to a panacea for well-being as we know.

Rituals and Routines and Faith

If strong rituals and routines are essential for personal and relationship well-being, they are essential for passing on the faith to our kids. In particular, we need to create a strong discipleship relationship with our children — that is, we need to create the kind of relationship with our kids that makes it natural for them to want to turn to us, listen to us, and receive instruction on how to live, love, and make decisions as Christians. And the key to creating this kind of healthy, compelling discipleship relationship with our children is strong, well-defined, regular, and frequent rituals and routines.

The family with strong *work rituals* — for instance, a regular expectation that family members will work together to clean the kitchen after dinner, or pick up the family room together before bed, or do various household projects together — learns virtues such as cooperation, teamwork, and trust. These virtues make children feel safe and cared for and more willing to listen to parents' advice and counsel, because they see from experience that following Mom and Dad's instructions leads to a more harmonious home life.

Play rituals — e.g., family game nights, family days, and special celebrations for birthdays, anniversaries, and the like — create a sense of joy, anticipation, and excitement about being together. Play rituals build your discipleship relationship by making deposits in the so-called relationship bank account. Metaphorically speaking, every time we offer compliments, give affection, or do something fun with our kids, we make deposits in the relationship bank account. By contrast, every time we correct our children or ask them to do chores or other work-related activities — especially if they aren't especially fun work activities — we make withdrawals from the relationship bank account. Research on marital relationships suggests that couples need to have twenty times more good, loving, supportive, pleasant interactions than they do negative, critical, or challenging exchanges in order for the relationship to be stable and happy (Gottmann, 2011). There is good reason to think this ratio holds up for other relationships—especially parent-child relationships—as well. People in general and children in particular behave better, are less likely to be disrespectful, and are more open to correction and instruction with people they feel happy and content to be around. Play rituals show our children that we can teach them not only how to follow rules and fulfill responsibilities but also how to enjoy themselves in healthful ways and experience life as a gift.

As you will see more clearly later in this book, children's faith development is largely both emotional and relational. For kids, if it feels good and builds relationships, it *is* good. If it feels bad and complicates relationships, it *is* bad. It doesn't matter what the objective truth of the situation is. Children are very black and white in this regard. They need to feel, in real and tangible ways, that you are able to show them how to live a joyful life. If going to church was all work and drudgery all the time—if there were never any celebrations, joyful moments, and enjoyable experiences—no one would go, and rightly so. If we are to create solid, engaging, discipleship relationships with our children, we need to follow God's example and make sure there is a strong element of fun and celebration involved, so that both we and our children learn that being in the presence of God and doing his will is the source of the greatest joy and happiness imaginable.

Talk rituals, such as meaningful family mealtimes, family walks, one-on-one dates with kids, and so forth, Pope Francis refers to as "wasting time with our children." We live in an age when "normal" family life consists almost entirely of conversations about who needs to be taken where and what needs to be picked up at the grocery store. Real conversations—thoughtful conversations—about our children's thoughts and feelings, hopes and dreams, fears, faults, failures, and deeper needs don't happen if we aren't intentional about making time for such discussions.

We are used to talking at our children, but discipleship relationships are mainly about listening. We tend not to think of it this way, but Catholic parents are in essence their children's spiritual directors. To be effective spiritual directors to our children, we need to create time simply to listen and learn what is important to them, what they are concerned about, what they are afraid of, what they hope for, and what is most important to them.

But children are terrible with "let's sit down and talk" time. They need conversations to emerge naturally from our interactions with them. When we carve out time to "do nothing" together—taking a walk, shooting hoops (not playing a game), going out for breakfast, or finding other excuses just to hang out with our kids—we create moments when it feels safe to begin discussing more personal topics. And—after a respectful period of time has passed to communicate that our kids have our full attention—when we ask direct questions about their lives and concerns, they are more likely to respond because they know that they will be heard. When we take the time to listen to our kids, they are more likely to listen to us, internalize our advice, and see the value of our counsel, because they will feel as if we really understand them and that our advice was meant for them and not something we said randomly to make us feel like parents.

Finally, *prayer rituals*, such as mealtime and bedtime prayers, giving children blessings, family prayer times, and attending church together, connect your family to God's grace and make God an important part of your everyday life together. Again, children are very experiential. They need to feel that God is a real and tangible part of their everyday life and not something added on as an afterthought. They can't see God, so in order to believe in him, they need to feel his presence. They need to experience God as someone who is involved intimately in the day-to-day life of your family. Regular prayer rituals make it possible to communicate all this to your children.

Making Rituals Count

In order for rituals and routines to have their full effect, they need to be intentional, regularly scheduled, and consistent. Ideally, families will carve out time for shorter opportunities to work, play, talk, and pray together every day and create somewhat larger opportunities for these activities each week.

Making time for these rituals of connection in your family will not only enable you to create truly deep and loving relationships with one another, and open up channels by which you can effectively communicate your faith, but it will also make your family a powerful witness of the importance of family life in God's plan of salvation.

The following exercise will help you use family rituals to create strong discipleship relationships between you and your children and to become a sign to the world of God's plan for family life. Don't worry if you can't do everything starting tomorrow. Just work through the exercise with an eye toward how you would like things to be. Then review the exercise in prayer every day, asking God to provide you with the grace and open the doors that will enable you to give proper place to your family — and to your responsibility to be your children's spiritual director.

Rituals and Routines

Work, Play, Talk, and Prayer Rituals Exercise

Consider the ways that you can make more of a concerted effort to carve our regular daily and weekly times to work, play, talk, and pray together as a family. Start small by noting the things you already do at least occasionally, and then add other ideas to round out what your discipleship relationship will look like in the family school of love and virtue.

Work rituals

Daily work rituals might include clearing the table together after dinner or cleaning up the family room together each evening. These rituals should take only five or ten minutes a day, but they are an important part of your family's ability to learn from each other. They are different from chores, which are more individual.

Weekly work rituals might include working in the yard together or doing some important household project with each other. Weekly work rituals might require an hour or so of your time together once or twice a week.

In the spaces below, write your daily and weekly work rituals and when you would ideally like to do them.

Our daily work rituals   When

_____

_____

_____

_____

Our weekly work rituals   When

_____

_____

_____

_____

Play rituals
Carve out ten to fifteen minutes for daily play rituals, which can include playing a short game, or wrestling together, or otherwise laughing and playing.

Weekly play rituals might involve a family game night or a family day after Sunday Mass and require an hour or more once or twice a week.

Write your daily and weekly play rituals below and when you might like to schedule them.

Our daily play rituals   When

_____

_____

_____

_____

Rituals and Routines

Our weekly play rituals   When

_____

_____

_____

_____

Talk rituals
Daily talk rituals might include a meaningful family meal or a walk together or some other activity that allows more significant conversations to evolve naturally.

Weekly talk rituals might include a parent-child date, breakfast out together, or sharing in some mutually enjoyable activity that offers the opportunity to "waste time together" and let conversations about thoughts and feelings, hopes and dreams, fears and faults, and deeper needs emerge as a matter of course.

Our daily talk rituals   When

_____

_____

_____

_____

Our weekly talk rituals   When

_____

_____

_____

_____

Prayer rituals
Daily prayer rituals might include mealtime prayers, bedtime prayers, praying over your children before school or other activities, family Bible reading, or discussions on faith topics. These should be activities that make God a part of your daily life and help you draw closer together as a family.

Weekly prayer rituals can include going to Mass together, taking time for adoration, a family Bible study, or a family catechism study, in which you learn and discuss the faith as a family for half an hour or so.

Our daily prayer rituals   When

_____

_____

_____

_____

Rituals and Routines

Our weekly prayer rituals   When

_____

_____

_____

_____

Family Rituals: Your Key to "Discipling" Your Children

Family rituals serve as the skeleton on which your entire family relationship hangs. They serve as the structures you need to make sure you are attending to all the important areas of your life together as a family. Family rituals make it possible to have deeper and more meaningful conversation and encounters with your children that give you the credibility you need to become your children's spiritual directors. Ultimately, family rituals become the means by which God communicates the grace of the sacrament of marriage and family life and allows you to experience him, up close and personal, in the day-to-day interactions you share.

Family rituals are the sacred rites of the domestic church that provide a graceful rhythm to your life together and enable you to encounter all the blessings that make life together the gift it was meant to be.

A Word about Holidays

Of course, when most people think about rituals, they think about holidays and all the various traditions that attend them. Sadly, as families have become separated geographically and people become more distant from their cultural traditions, many families have even lost their holiday rituals. When we were children, for example, it would have been unthinkable to go to a movie on Christmas Day. There were too many rituals to attend to at home between church and the family meal and the various traditions that we enjoyed within our nuclear and extended families. Today, of course, the biggest movies of the season are released on Christmas Day because film companies know that something has to fill the void that family celebrations once occupied.

Christians must lead the charge in reestablishing the primacy of family rituals for holidays and seasons, especially Christmas and Easter but also Advent, Lent, Holy Week, holy days of obligation[2] and important saints' feast days (such as those of St. Patrick, St. Joseph, our patron saints, and so forth).

There are some wonderful books on this topic. For instance, *The Catholic Home* by Meredith Gould is a terrific look at common Catholic celebrations throughout the year, as is *The Big Book of Catholic Customs and Traditions* by Anne E. Neuberger.

Reclaim your family identity. Celebrate the daily, weekly, and holiday rituals that make your domestic church a joyful place where you all join together in service of a common identity and remind each other to experience life as the gift from God that it is meant to be.

---

[2] In the United States, the holy days of obligation are the solemnity of Mary, the Mother of God (January 1); the Ascension of Jesus (forty days after Easter); the Assumption of Mary (August 15); All Saints' Day (November 1); the Immaculate Conception (December 8); and Christmas (December 25).

4

Go and Make Disciples of Your Children:
Creating Discipleship Hearts

In chapter 3, we discussed how family rituals serve as the skeleton of the discipleship relationship you need to have with your children in order to help them see the relevance of God and your faith in their everyday lives. But while making time for family rituals is critical for creating a discipleship relationship with your children, you will also need to open your children's hearts to these activities—and much more besides—so that they will be willing participants and will actively seek all the blessings they can receive from these times together with you.

We regularly hear from families who try to schedule game nights or prayer times or some other regular family ritual, only to have it end in bickering, bitterness, and tears. Part of this can be solved by making a commitment to these rituals and sticking to it through any initial resistance, but the other part is to make sure that your children have a healthy attachment to the life of your family; that you have taught your children how to have the heart of a disciple.

A child with a discipleship heart is one who displays the characteristics of openness, affection, cheerful obedience, and playfulness.

- *Openness:* he willingly receives and often requests your advice on personal or emotional topics and takes what you say to heart. Openness is an essential ingredient for discipleship because it enables your child to be receptive to your example and your instruction.

- *Affection:* he initiates affection with you and willingly and comfortably receives the affection you offer him (he melts into it instead of being stiff or wiggly or pulling away). Affection is an essential ingredient of discipleship because it speaks to the strength of your connection with your child. A child who willingly receives and actively seeks your affection and approval is a child whose heart is open to deeper relationship with you and with the God you serve.

- *Cheerful obedience:* a child who is cheerfully obedient will do what is asked of him without resistance and look for opportunities to do things, on his own, to serve you and the family. Cheerful obedience is a sign of strong rapport between you and your child, a rapport that makes him want to work to please you even when what you ask of him is difficult and requires some degree of sacrifice.

- *Playfulness:* a playful child accepts your invitation to do fun things and enjoys time with you. He also takes the initiative to do and share things with you. Playfulness is essential to discipleship because it is a sign that your child acknowledges you as a person who has the ability to teach him to experience and live life as a joyful gift.

The more a child exhibits these qualities in his day-to-day interactions with you, the more you can say that you have been successful in creating a discipleship relationship with your child. The good news is, regardless of the degree to which your child displays these qualities, there is much that you, as a parent, can do to cultivate them.

Attachment: The Source of Discipleship

Fostering a discipleship heart means more than making sure our children have ears to hear. It means making sure they have hearts that desire to be formed; hearts that make them turn toward us and say, "Teach me."

Psychologists have found that what we are calling a discipleship heart is rooted in the idea of attachment. Attachment is understood as the strength of the child's impulse to turn toward his caregiver to get his needs met (Neufeld and Maté, 2008). It is the degree to which a child feels, in his gut, that his parents are the people to whom he can turn whenever he has a question or needs to learn how to meet a need or is struggling to solve a problem. The strength of this impulse in a child determines whether his attachment style is *secure, anxious,* or *avoidant* (Ainsworth and Bell, 1970).

A child with a strong, *secure* attachment style has an innate, bone-deep, almost irresistible impulse to see his parents as the people who are best equipped to teach him how to meet his emotional, spiritual, and relational needs in godly and efficient ways. The securely attached child knows that one day he will stand on his own, and although he is eager to do so, he also knows that the best way to accomplish this goal is to walk in his parents' footsteps and learn the walk of life from them by attending carefully to what they say and do. Researchers note that securely attached children are capable of deep and satisfying relationships with God. They work hard to make good choices, but they are confident in God's mercy when they fall, and they find it generally easy to trust in God's constant love and providence.

By contrast, a child with an *anxious* attachment style tends to doubt that his parents are a reliable source of information. Because of this, he usually turns to multiple people and sources to seek their opinions as well and ends up confused and uncertain about what to do. The anxiously attached child has many masters and is always trying to please them all. This prevents him from being able to know his own mind or being confident about whom to turn to for authoritative help. Psychologists observe that anxiously attached children tend to want a relationship with God but are often nervous that he will abandon them if they try his patience too much or don't toe the line. They often have a deep sense of a need for God but are afraid to trust him. Rather than trusting in God's providence, they often feel that although God took care of them last time, he may not be there the next time. And even if they feel guilty about it, they often resent the blessings he gives others, fearing that there may not be enough grace to go around.

Finally, the child with an *avoidant* attachment style believes that it is pointless to ask his parents—or anyone else, for that matter—how to meet his emotional, spiritual, or relational needs. He tends to resist, ignore, or outright reject input from others and tries to figure everything out on his own, often with less than desirable results. Child psychologists note that avoidantly attached children tend to think of relationships with people as something of a mystery, to say nothing of a relationship with God. They tend not to share their thoughts or feelings openly with anyone, and as a result, they are also not usually interested in cultivating a prayer life or a meaningful personal relationship with God. If they do manage to be religious, their faith is usually rooted not in love but in duty, following the rules and the expectation that they will be rewarded for their faithful service. If things don't go their way or they experience even normal setbacks in life they are quick to become angry — at both others and God — for not holding up their end of the "deal."

Attachment and Discipleship:
What's a Parent to Do?

So, are children born with their attachment style? No, researchers universally say. Attachment styles are firmly rooted in how promptly, consistently, and generously children *feel their parents have responded to their needs over the years.* God designed the family so that parents would be his face to their children. The degree to which a child feels that his parents met his needs *generously, promptly, and consistently* is the degree to which the child will develop a secure attachment to his parents.

The harder a child has to work to feel heard, to feel taken seriously by his mom and dad, or to find a sympathetic ear with his parents, the more insecure the attachment will be from the child to the parent. That attachment relationship becomes the child's *internal working model* — the unconscious gut-level, a priori assumptions he brings into all relationships, including his relationship with God. A child who enjoys the kind of relationship with his parents that reflects the mission of the Catholic family we discussed earlier, one in which he experiences "a sense of justice, cordial openness, dialogue, generous service, solidarity and all the other values which help people to live life as a gift," is a child who will most certainly develop a secure attachment relationship first with his parents and then with others and with God.

The child who has to work harder, cry longer, or wait longer to get his parents' attention and affection and get his needs met in general will tend to have more of an anxious attachment and will tend to worry about alienating or being abandoned by God. Because it has always been the child's job to find the right combination of behaviors to get his parents' attention and his emotional needs met, he has a tendency to blame himself for any problems in intimate relationships, even when the problems aren't his fault. This includes his relationship with God, where the anxiously attached person tends toward scrupulosity and the fear that he could do something to make God stop loving him or abandon him. He might struggle to be honest with God about his failings and difficulties and have a hard time trusting in God's providence and mercy.

The child whose emotional and relational needs are largely ignored, who is raised in a home with little affection or emotional communication will develop a more *avoidant* attachment style. Because it was always the child's job to take care of himself, he might tend to struggle with anger in relationships and with the fear of being taken advantage of, or he might simply not see why he should need other people at all. In his spiritual life, he might struggle with either a deep anger at God for not playing by the rules when things don't go his way or might never think to reach out to God in the first place, since he is used to taking care of himself.

It's important to note that the key to good attachment is how hard the child *feels* he has to work to be heard and get his needs met. Almost all parents think they are doing a great — or at least good enough — job of responding to their children's needs. That is irrelevant. To get a sense of the strength of your children's attachment to you, ask yourself how quickly, generously, and consistently *your children* would say you respond to them and their needs—and how hard they have to work to get you to listen to them and help them get what they want. That will give you a better sense of how the process of "discipling" your child is going for you.

Attachment Isn't Spoiling

Attachment does not mean that you have to give your children everything they want, when they want it, and how they want it. It means listening to them, taking the time to understand why they want the things they want, and—if you can't let them have those things they want how and when they want them—brainstorming more godly and efficient ways that you could help them meet at least some of those needs in the here and now.

Alternatively, if you have to say no, as parents often must, it is always for a good and objective reason (for instance, your child's safety or well-being) and not just because you don't feel like it or because you reactively tend to say no to things out of stress and irritability.

In infancy and toddlerhood, fostering healthy attachment means responding promptly, generously, and consistently to cries. It means trusting the schedule God has built into your child for sleeping, feeding, and comforting and not making your child "cry it out" at night or cry for long periods as a matter of habit during the day. Crying is never good for a child. It always means he needs help in regulating some system in his body (Sunderland, 2008). God gives parents the responsibility to attend to those cries promptly, just as he tells us he does in Psalm 34:4. "I sought the LORD, and he answered me, and delivered me from all my fears."

As your child matures through childhood and adolescence, his needs become more complicated to meet. Parents should, as much as possible, use the "qualified-yes" technique in responding to these needs unless the request is for something that is truly contrary to the child's well-being. For instance, if a child asked for something the parent couldn't afford, the qualified-yes technique would have the parent say, "I can afford to contribute only X toward that, but let's talk about ways you might be able to earn the difference if it is that important to you. Otherwise, this is what I can do. What do you think?" This would be as opposed to saying, for instance, "You want me to spend $250 on a pair of sneakers? Are you crazy?"

With the qualified-yes technique, the child learns that the parent is always someone to whom he can turn to get help in meeting his needs or making a plan by which those needs could be met. Because of this, even when the parent can't supply what the child wants or needs, the child still feels attached because he has been heard and helped to come up with a plan. And, if the child decides that having that thing really isn't worth the effort after all, it is he who makes that decision, and not the parent who makes himself an obstacle to achieving that need or want. (For more on how to use the qualified-yes technique as a way of fostering attachment through childhood and adolescence, check out our book *Parenting with Grace: The Catholic Parents' Guide to Raising [Almost] Perfect Kids.*)

Taking Attachment to the World

Again, there is universal agreement in the research on the psychology of faith development that responding promptly, generously, and consistently to a child's needs—even when the parent cannot, ultimately, grant that particular need—is absolutely critical to developing a healthy internal working model of relationships that enables the child to have a positive, trusting relationship with God. It is difficult to overestimate just how important this parent-child dynamic is for passing on the faith to our children. One recently released study followed almost 3,500 individuals in 350 families over the course of forty years to see what factors were most important for passing on the faith from one generation to the next. In all the data, the number-one factor that contributed to children's "catching" the faith of their parents was *parental warmth* (Bengtson, 2013). The warmth with which you receive your child's requests and the openness you display toward your child's needs — from the first cries in infancy and toddlerhood to requests for greater responsibility and independence in adolescence — set the stage for the warmth he projects onto his relationship with God and the eagerness with which he can be expected to turn to God in good times and bad.

The degree of warmth you display toward your child in general and his needs and requests in particular establish your child's attachment style, the subconscious gut-level assumptions he brings into every relationship. Because these assumptions are so ingrained and subconscious, it is difficult to change them, once they have been established, without great effort. It is possible to heal a child's attachment style so that it becomes more secure, but doing so is akin to having to repair the foundation of your house while you're still living in it. It can be done, but no one wants to have to do it if he can avoid it. Better to give your child the security he needs from day one by cultivating his discipleship heart and letting him know that when he cries out at any age, you will be there to answer him and help him find godly, efficient ways to meet his needs.

Attachment-to-God Inventory

As you read through this chapter, you may have some questions about your own relationship with God. Knowing your own attachment style and how it impacts your relationship with God can be tremendously important. First, we tend to assume that whatever our attachment style is—however insecure it may be—it represents the "normal" way people "ought" to relate to others and to God. This causes us potentially to limit our expectations of how close we should draw to God. But God wants to tear down all the walls between him and us and achieve total union with his children (see John 17:21). We must always strive toward greater dependence on God and security in our relationship to God.

Secondly, we tend to communicate these same expectations—however limited they may be—to our children. In this way, without even knowing it, we communicate to our children our own attachment style and our gut-level assumptions about God. The following quiz can help you evaluate your attachment style and begin to consider how you can grow in your relationship with God as you and your children discover God together.

The following quiz is a statistically valid and reliable measure that evaluates the degree to which a person's relationship with God is healthy and secure. Most people are surprised by the results. How do you score?

"ATTACHMENT TO GOD" INVENTORY[3]

Directions: Circle the number that indicates your level of agreement, from *disagree strongly* (DS) to *neutral* (N) to *agree strongly*

---

[3] R. Beck and A. McDonald, "Attachment to God Inventory," *Journal of Psychology and Theology* 32, no. 2 (2004): 92–103.

(AS). The points assigned will vary from question to question. Don't worry about the numbers for now; just view them as place-holders that indicate your level of agreement or disagreement with each question.

1. My experiences with God are very intimate and emotional.

DS			N			AS
7	6	5	4	3	2	1

2. I prefer not to depend too much on God.

DS			N			AS
7	6	5	4	3	2	1

3. My prayers to God are very emotional.

DS			N			AS
7	6	5	4	3	2	1

4. I am totally dependent on God for everything in my life.

DS			N			AS
7	6	5	4	3	2	1

5. Without God I couldn't function at all.

DS			N			AS
7	6	5	4	3	2	1

6. I just don't feel a deep need to be close to God.

DS			N			AS
7	6	5	4	3	2	1

7. Daily I discuss all my problems and concerns with God.

DS			N			AS
7	6	5	4	3	2	1

8. I am uncomfortable allowing God to control every aspect of my life.

DS			N			AS
7	6	5	4	3	2	1

9. I let God make most of the decisions in my life.

DS			N			AS
7	6	5	4	3	2	1

10. I am uncomfortable with emotional displays of affection toward God.

DS			N			AS
7	6	5	4	3	2	1

11. It is uncommon for me to cry when sharing with God.

DS			N			AS
7	6	5	4	3	2	1

12. I am uncomfortable being emotional in my communication with God.

DS			N			AS
7	6	5	4	3	2	1

13. I believe people should not depend on God for things they should do for themselves.

DS			N			AS
7	6	5	4	3	2	1

14. My prayers to God are often matter-of-fact and not very personal.

DS			N			AS
7	6	5	4	3	2	1

Subtotal Scale 1 (questions 1–14) _____

15. I worry a lot about my relationship with God.

DS			N			AS
7	6	5	4	3	2	1

16. I often worry about whether God is pleased with me.

DS			N			AS
7	6	5	4	3	2	1

17. I get upset when I feel God helps others but forgets about me.

DS			N			AS
7	6	5	4	3	2	1

18. I fear God does not accept me when I do wrong.

DS			N			AS
7	6	5	4	3	2	1

19. I often feel angry with God for not responding to me.

DS			N			AS
7	6	5	4	3	2	1

20. I worry a lot about damaging my relationship with God.

DS			N			AS
7	6	5	4	3	2	1

21. I am jealous at how God seems to care more for others than for me.

DS			N			AS
7	6	5	4	3	2	1

22. I am jealous when others feel God's presence when I cannot.

DS			N			AS
7	6	5	4	3	2	1

23. I am jealous at how close some people are to God.

DS			N			AS
7	6	5	4	3	2	1

24. If I can't see God working in my life, I get upset or angry.

DS			N			AS
7	6	5	4	3	2	1

25. Sometimes I feel as if God loves others more than me.

DS			N			AS
7	6	5	4	3	2	1

26. Almost daily I feel that my relationship with God goes back and forth from "hot" to "cold."

DS			N			AS
7	6	5	4	3	2	1

27. I crave reassurance from God that God loves me.

DS			N			AS
7	6	5	4	3	2	1

28. Even if I fail, I never question that God is pleased with me.

DS			N			AS
7	6	5	4	3	2	1

Subtotal Scale 2 (questions 15–28) _____

Grand Total of Scales 1 and 2 (questions 1–28) _____

Scoring

Step 1: Add the points for all the questions. This is your Overall "Attachment to God" Score. This score suggests how secure your relationship with God is overall. The *lower* the score, the better. The lowest possible score is a 28 (1 point per question) which would indicate an "absolutely secure" relationship with God. Very few people, if any, achieve this low a score. A score of 56 or less still indicates a "very secure" relationship with God. Scores higher than 57 (up to a maximum of 196) may indicate varying degrees of insecurity in your relationship with God. That insecurity could cause you to be more anxious about or avoidant in your relationship with God than you ought to be. Steps 2 and 3 will help you determine which (avoidance or anxiety) is more responsible for the degree of insecurity you display.

Step 2: Add your numbers from questions 1 through 14. Write the total on the line marked "Subtotal Scale 1." This is your score for the Avoidant "Attachment to God" Scale. The *lower* the score, the better. The lowest possible score is 14, which would indicate that you are not at all avoidant in your relationship with God. In other words, you feel *absolutely eager* to share your thoughts, feelings, hopes, and dreams with God and to rely on him in every aspect of your life. A score of 28 or less suggests that you are generally very comfortable sharing your thoughts, feelings, hopes, and dreams with God and relying on him in every aspect of your life. A score of 29 or higher means that there might be several ways you tend to resist sharing your heart with God or relying on him in parts of your life. The higher your Avoidant Scale score, the more obstacles you tend to put up between yourself and God and the harder it is for you to let him influence your life and relationships. The maximum possible score on the Avoidant Scale is 98.

Step 3: Add your numbers to questions 15 through 28, and write the total on the line marked "Subtotal Scale 2." This is your score for the Anxious "Attachment to God" Scale. The *lower* the score, the better. The lowest possible score is 14, which would indicate that you are absolutely confident and trusting in your relationship with God. In other words, you never doubt or question God's mercy, providence, or caring and nurturing presence in your life. A score of 28 or less suggests that you rarely doubt or question God's mercy, providence, or caring and nurturing presence in your life. A score of 29 or higher means that you tend to worry that God might not always be there for you, that you might behave in ways that could cause him to abandon you, or that somehow he might forget about you and your needs. The higher your Anxious Scale score, the stronger your anxiety is that God might either forget or abandon you or that you might alienate him with even simple mistakes or errors in judgment (i.e., scrupulosity). The maximum possible score on the Anxious Scale is 98.

What Does Your Score Mean, and What Can You Do?

If you scored higher on the Avoidant Scale: In order to be able to pass the healthiest relationship with God on to your children, you will need to make an intentional effort to share more of your own life with God. Make a point of talking to him about your hopes, dreams, fears, concerns, and joys. It will probably feel silly or unnecessary. Do it anyway. God wants to be part of every aspect of your life. He wants to be one with you (see John 17:21). It will take effort to remind yourself that you need God. Cultivate the discipline of prayer and especially of sharing your concerns, even though you tend to feel as if everything is up to you in your life. You don't have to feel so alone any more. Learn to fight against the self-talk that causes you to believe that you don't or shouldn't need God's help. Jesus is standing at the door of your heart and knocking. Make the consistent effort to let him in. A spiritual director or pastoral counselor can be helpful to you in keeping you accountable for opening your heart appropriately to God.

If you scored higher on the Anxious Scale: In order to pass the healthiest relationship with God on to your children, you will need to make an intentional effort to remind yourself of God's past providence, mercy, and steadfast love. Keep a gratitude journal to recall the blessings of each day. Likewise write down the times that God has delivered you from past difficulties, and review this list in prayer often—perhaps daily. Reflect on passages in Scripture that remind you of your ability to trust in God. Learn to fight against the self-talk that tells you that you are unworthy of God's love or that you could ever do anything that could make God stop loving and caring for you. A spiritual director or pastoral counselor can help you find your confidence in God's fidelity when you are struggling to find your spiritual center.

Conclusion

Throughout *Discovering God Together* we hope to show you that you are not just leading your children closer to God, but God is also calling out to you through your children and inviting you into a deeper relationship with him. Most of us experience at least some degree of insecurity—either anxiousness or avoidance—in our relationship with God. By working to heal that tendency in our relationship with our children, we ultimately open our hearts to God, our heavenly Father, and he teaches us, his children, how to receive all the grace, blessing, and love he wants to pour into our hearts. Part of discipling our children means learning to be better disciples ourselves. The more we cultivate our secure attachment to God and help our children develop a secure attachment to us, the stronger a discipleship heart will beat in the very life of our family and the more effective we can be at discovering God, and all of his grace and bounty, together.

5

Shepherding Kids through the Stages of Faith

The Church teaches us that there are three virtues that God gives us as gifts: faith, hope, and love. These three qualities are a natural and essential part of our humanness. It takes work to develop them, but they are always present as a basic part of our humanity. Psychology bears this out. Hope is the virtue that empowers us to believe that growth, healing, change, and justice are possible even in the face of overwhelming evidence to the contrary. Hope is an essential part of our human nature that drives us forward. If we lose hope, we despair and die, but if we retain hope, we can face and overcome anything.

Love is the virtue that makes us want to share ourselves with others and create connection with those around us. Love is an innate human need that is more basic than food. If a baby does not feel loved, he will develop a condition called *failure to thrive* and will die, but if a child is loved well and generously, he can achieve deep, soulful satisfaction in his life and relationships.

Faith is similarly an innate human experience. Even before it is expressed as belief in anything, faith is the irresistible drive to seek beyond ourselves for significance, for truth, meaning, and purpose. It is the natural impulse that says, "There is something out there that is more than me, and I must seek it to be fulfilled."

Stages of Faith

In this most basic sense, faith first expresses itself as the baby reaches out for the mother's breast and cries out for help in the night. It is this basic sense of faith that makes the child call out, "I know I am not enough on my own. There is something greater than me out there! I'm crying out. Who will answer?"

From this first relationship, the child's natural sense of basic faith—that basic human drive for making meaning, for significance, for purpose, and for connection with "the other"—grows as the child makes more connections first with people, then with stories and rituals, then with a community, and finally with ever-deepening stages of personal belief and conversion.

Psychologist Dr. James Fowler (1995) observed that this basic, innately human kind of faith that we are discussing evolves in stages. At each stage, the person requires a slightly different type of spiritual food to nurture him through that stage into the next one. Children—indeed, people of all ages—who receive the correct kind of spiritual nourishment at each stage come to exhibit an increasingly deep, intimate, robust, and personal faith life, filled with a meaningful and rich system of harmonious, life-affirming beliefs, whereas people who are deprived of that proper spiritual nourishment experience a faith life that stalls at a particular stage or withers and even dies, tearing down whatever belief had begun to flower on faith's vine.

Fowler's research identifies seven *stages of faith*. Knowing these stages and the kind of spiritual nourishment your child needs at each one will help you nurture the seeds God has planted in your child's heart, enabling him to produce a harvest of thirty- or sixty- or a hundredfold (see Matt. 13:8–9). Even though you will most likely nurture your child only through the first four stages (the remaining three are usually reserved for adulthood), we will briefly examine all seven stages so that you can also get a sense of your own stage of faith. Parents cannot give what they do not have. As we discover God together, we will need to stay at least a stage or two ahead of our children in order for them to consider us to be credible mentors to them on their spiritual journey.

Here are the seven stages of faith (please note that age ranges are approximate).

1. Primal Faith (birth through age two)

2. Gut-Level Feeling/Projective Faith (ages three through seven)

3. Story-Based Faith (school age through adult)

4. Relationship-Based Faith (age twelve through adult)

5. Personal Faith (adulthood and on)

6. Integrated Faith (middle adulthood and on)

7. Universalizing Faith (later adulthood)

Most of these approximate age ranges represent at what age that particular stage of faith becomes possible. That said, there are many adults whose faith never moves beyond stage 3 or 4, even though these stages theoretically "come online" in middle childhood and adolescence, respectively. It takes effort to develop one's capacity for making meaning and seeking significance. If you don't work at it, or haven't been discipled properly, your faith development could stall and you could remain at a childish stage of faith development for the rest of your life, not knowing that there was any more for you. The rest of the chapter will briefly describe each stage and what you can do to feed your own and your child's faith at that stage.

Discovering God Together

Stage 1: Primal Faith

This is the stage we were mostly dealing with in our last chapter on attachment and attachment styles. The infant and toddler aren't concerned with big questions about life, the universe, and everything, but they are concerned with basic questions such as: "When I call, who will come? Can I count on them to come consistently? Can I count on them to respond generously? Can I be confident that when I call, someone will always come?" These simple questions form the child's basic "internal working model" that represents the level of confidence the child feels he can display in all his relationships and ultimately his relationship with God. The degree to which parents respond to their child's needs promptly, consistently, and generously will determine whether their child will develop a secure, anxious, or avoidant posture toward all relationships, including his relationship with God.

At this stage, parents can best facilitate their child's faith development by modeling the kind of parenthood God tells us he displays toward us. Scripture tells us repeatedly that when we call, God answers our cries promptly, generously, and consistently (see Ps. 91:15). He meets all our needs (see Phil. 4:19). We can always count on his love and caretaking (see Ps. 136:1). God responds to us even before our cry can leave our lips (see Isa. 65:24)! When parents respond to their child's needs promptly, generously, and consistently, they not only model God's loving kindness and providence; they also teach their child to be confident in God's care.

Stage 2: Gut-Level Feeling/Projective Faith
(Ages Three through Seven)

If basic faith is best understood as the human drive for making meaning and seeking significance, this is the stage where the child's efforts to do this become obvious to parents. At this stage, the child doesn't really intellectually understand concepts such as "God the Father" or "Jesus" or "Holy Spirit" or "angels" or "saints" but is learning how to *feel* about them and toward them. Do I feel warmly toward these beings I can't see (secure attachment)? Am I excited about them (secure), or do they make me a little nervous (anxious attachment)? Do I feel angry or fearful toward them because they are always "watching me" (anxious or avoidant), or do I take comfort in this fact (secure)?

Children at this stage begin to take the internal working model they developed in stage 1 and apply it to the otherworldly beings whom parents introduce to them through stories, prayer times, rituals, and worship. Although, by teaching children about Bible stories, saint stories, fables, and morals, parents are setting the groundwork for future understanding, at this stage, children's focus is primarily on learning how to feel about God, saints and angels, and their faith community in general. Because of this, so-lidifying family rituals—especially happy, relationship-building rituals around family prayer, spiritual reading, and worship—is tremendously important.

To facilitate faith development at this stage, parents should make family prayer times as "cuddly" (yes, cuddly) as possible, having the child sit in your lap. Sing children's Bible songs and other age-appropriate praise-and-worship songs, and focus on prayers that emphasize how much God loves them and the family, how he has taken care of them and the family that day, and how he wants us to love him back with all our heart. If you are prone to bristle at this warmer, fuzzier approach to prayer, remember that the *Catechism of the Catholic Church* teaches that prayer is a call to intimate communion with God *and* each other (no. 2565). Prayer has both vertical (divine relationship) and horizontal (human relationship) dimensions. Before a child can fully appreciate the vertical dimensions of prayer, he has to have a solid sense that prayer time is a warm, safe, loving, and joyful experience that is beneficial on the horizontal, family-relationship level.

Likewise, at this stage, singing songs about God, engaging in faith rituals, and reading Bible stories, appropriate saint stories, and other moral or ethical fables is less about learning the lessons and concepts such stories teach as about learning the lesson that "reading, talking, and doing God-things means getting to spend time with Mommy and Daddy, and that feels good!" That's why taking a gentle approach to helping kids pay attention and stay focused on prayer and faith activities is so important. Of course, it is important to use gentle approaches to discipline in general, but it is especially important at prayer times and Mass (see *Parenting with Grace* for more ideas on general approaches to effective gentle discipline). The focus of any discipline during Mass and prayer times should be on maintaining basic order and focus, as opposed to lockstep compliance and rigid attention.

In addition to basic, loving family rituals for prayer and worship, faith-based toys and dolls, craft projects, coloring books, and picture books offer wonderful forms of faith development at this stage. The goal is not so much to teach the child the facts of the faith (although there is nothing wrong with this to the degree that it's possible) as it is to teach the child that learning about the faith is a good, warm, joyful, intimate, interesting and even fun thing to do.

Stage 3: Story-Based Faith (School Age through Adult)

In this stage, the child begins to attach greater intellectual meaning to the Bible stories, saint stories, and moral fables that were primarily a source of emotional comfort. Children ages seven and older have achieved basic reasoning ability, so their capacity for making meaning and seeking significance reaches a new level. The stories they once enjoyed hearing now become the foundation for intellectual faith and moral development. Children at this age begin to understand that stories are more just than a source of entertainment and emotional connection with caregivers; they are an important place to turn to learn life lessons and ways of being and behaving. The story about Jesus healing the ten lepers is no longer just a story about how loving Jesus is; it is also a story about being thankful for the blessings God gives. Aesop's fable about the ant and the grasshopper is no longer just a story about a grumpy ant and a silly grasshopper. It is a tale of responsibility and the importance of delayed gratification.

At this stage of faith (which encompasses both young children and many adults) people can be rather literal about the stories that form the foundations of their faith; in fact, Fowler referred to this stage of faith as the Mythic-Literal Stage. In adulthood, Story-Based Faith can be a positive, simple, dutiful sense of faith rooted in a person who, for whatever reason, never learned to ask deeper questions about the greater significance of the Bible stories he heard as a child. Or it could be much more pathological in the form of a very us-versus-them tribalism that elevates liturgical preferences and overly strict interpretations of religious and moral texts that lead to violent battles within and between faith groups. Religious fundamentalists are often stuck at this stage of faith development.

For children, of course, Story-Based Faith is a necessary and important faith stage. At this point, parents do well to discuss the deeper personal and moral significance of the different stories they tell their children about their faith. Asking questions about what a story means, or what Jesus was trying to say to us in a particular parable or what we can learn from the example of a certain saint can be very helpful at this age, as such questions help maximize children's meaning-making capacity with regard to faith stories. Parents need to understand that stories, for this age group, are not merely stories. They are life lessons. The truths conveyed by these stories become the intellectual and emotional foundation for the way our children make major life decisions, the way our children think about relationships and understand their place in the world. Children of this age need stories to develop a clear sense of who they are. If Christian parents do not tell their children Bible stories, saint stories, and other stories that support moral development and the attainment of virtue, children will simply gravitate toward and absorb the stories that are available to them: the stories they hear from television, pop music, and their friends. The stories parents tell at this age form the basis of their children's worldview for the rest of their lives.

Exploring the biblical basis for why Catholics do what we do, think as we think, and pray as we pray (an activity known as apologetics) with your children can be a very useful activity at this stage. There are several apologetics resources for children that fit the bill: Matt Pinto's *Friendly Defenders* cards and Amy Welborn's *Prove It!* series of books can lead to great faith discussions in the home that can engage both parents and children and help families discover God together in intellectually appealing ways.

It can also be helpful, to a limited degree, to ask slightly harder questions for reflection that place superficially contradictory stories side by side and ask children to consider what the deeper truths might be. For instance, reading the parable of the prodigal son (which attests to God's infinite mercy) followed by the parable of the unmerciful servant (which shows God dealing rather harshly with those who do not show mercy) can lead to interesting discussions with children about when are we expected to be merciful to others and when is it okay to hold others accountable for their actions. Or, for that matter, reading the story of Noah and the Flood (in which God wipes all but one family off the face of the earth because of the sinfulness of mankind) followed by the story of the Good Shepherd (in which God goes to great lengths to save one lost sheep) can lead to interesting conversations about how love and justice go together. It is okay if you or your children don't come up with definitive answers to these paradoxes, as there often aren't definitive answers — although it's always good to seek additional advice or counsel from books or your pastor when questions come up. At this stage of the game, teaching your children that faith stories (1) contain moral and spiritual truths and (2) are often more rich and complex than they appear at first reading will help your children get the most out of this stage of faith and prepare them for the next.

In addition to verbal discussions and storytelling, tangible reminders of your faith can be very important at this stage. Catholicism is full of sacramentals: statues, crucifixes, prayer cards, religious jewelry and art, holy water, scapulars, and the like. These physical signs of God's grace can help you stay connected to your faith throughout your life, but they can be an especially important aid to children at this stage of faith development. Sacramentals are never to be thought of as talismans, but they do serve as a connection to God and as a reminder of God's presence in our lives, and as such, they do have a certain power to make our faith life more real and tangible. Children, especially, love these physical reminders of God's grace. Setting up a prayer corner for your child with a special picture or statue of Jesus, or giving him a medal of his patron saint, or having him kiss Jesus' feet on the crucifix and say, "I love you, Jesus" each day when he wakes up or before he goes to bed are just a few important ways for children at this stage to develop deep, meaningful, and personal connections with their developing faith.

Finally, it is important to help cultivate your child's personal prayer life at this stage. We will discuss how to do this later in the book, but we mention it here because this is when learning good personal prayer habits are most natural and important.

Stage 4: Relationship-Based Faith
(Adolescence through Adulthood)

Relationship-Based Faith (or Synthetic-Conventional Faith, as Fowler calls it) makes an appearance during the teen years, although it is very common for most adults to remain at this stage of faith throughout their lives. This is the point at which people discover the social dimension of faith. For the first time, the faith stories that gave meaning and structure to the child's life are seen not just in terms of rules for living but as a means of achieving deeper intimacy and connection with others.

For the person (adolescent or adult) at this stage of faith, religion is understood to be "good" to the degree that it facilitates the person's relationships with others and "bad" to the degree that it complicates the person's relationships with others. If this seems off-putting and somehow "unspiritual," remember that the entire purpose of the Christian walk is union with God and the Communion of Saints. Faith is supposed to call us into deeper relationship with God and others. This is the stage at which people begin to discover this relational/communal aspect of faith on the broader level.

Assuming the child has gotten a good sense of how his family's faith has been the source of joy, intimacy, love, fellowship, and peace in his home, he is now at the stage when he wants to see how his faith guides his interactions with the wider world. This is the first time many families run into serious challenges with their children's faith development and experience resistance to religious formation or even rejection of it altogether. This resistance is often caused by the child's comparing the quality of his relationships within the family to the quality of relationships in the world and finding his family relationships lacking in some way.

For instance, if the child sees that the relationships in his erstwhile faithful family are no happier or healthier — or, worse, are even less loving and harmonious — than the relationships in families of a different faith or of no faith at all, that child may come to see his parents as hypocrites and reject the faith that has been communicated to him as "just a bunch of rules" that don't have anything to do with "real life."

Another complication can arise if the child did not receive adequate exposure to the idea of paradox that we discussed in the last stage. For instance, if the child was told that "sex outside of marriage is bad" but not given the opportunity to understand that doing the wrong thing doesn't necessarily make people bad people, he may come to reject his faith when his friends begin having premarital sex. After all, "my parents said that only bad people do those things and I always felt that way too, but my friends are having sex, and I know my friends aren't bad people. The Church must be wrong." Today, we often see the same thing about homosexuality and gay marriage, "My parents said that homosexuality is bad, and I always thought so. But last week my friend [or brother or cousin] just came out, and he's a really nice person. And now, he's hurting and scared. The Church must be wrong." While there are legitimate questions to be asked about these complicated moral situations, people at this stage rarely get to those discussions because they are so focused on the relational impact of their childhood faith.

Again, people at this stage often fail to appreciate the objective dimensions of faith and morals and believe that faith is good to the degree that it fosters relationships and makes people feel welcome and is bad to the degree that it complicates relationships and makes people feel excluded. If children have not been given sufficient opportunity to wrestle with the kinds of paradoxes we referenced in the last stage by at least the preteen years, it can be very difficult to begin such discussions now because the child's focus has changed from learning how to think about faith matters to learning how to apply the way he already thinks to his social sphere.

Regardless, there are four things parents can do to help their children receive all the benefits they can from this stage of faith and move on to the next, more mature and personal stage of faith in young adulthood.

1. *Recenter faith as the source of family intimacy.* The child who is raised in a home where he has experienced the faith as a source of greater intimacy, joy, love, peace, and togetherness than his friends — especially his different-faith and no-faith friends — experience in their homes tends to retain his faith even when his family's rules bring him into conflict with his peers. By contrast, the parents whose child sees that "my friends' families don't get along any worse — or get along much better — than my family, and *they're allowed to go to that party [or see that movie or go drinking or have sex with their boyfriends or girlfriends]*" might be in for a rough ride. By contrast, children who have experienced the morals and rules of their faith as leading to a deeper, richer, more

loving family life are willing to adhere and even defend at least many of the more challenging rules or morals to their friends because they see how much better off they are because of those rules and morals.

If a family hasn't created the kinds of strong rituals and routines or worked hard to cultivate the kind of attachment and togetherness we mentioned earlier in the book, it will be important to do whatever is possible to build those rituals and connections now as much as possible. This includes rituals that cultivate the good personal prayer habits that we mentioned in the last stage but which we'll discuss extensively in a later chapter.

Of course, families who have been working hard at these tasks will want to make sure they find ways to keep up those rituals — and perhaps occasionally include their children's friends in those rituals — even while their child is looking for ways to spend time with peers. This is the single most important principle to remember to help your teen successfully negotiate the Relationship Stage of faith development.

2. Parents must disciple teens' relationships with goals and desires. Obviously, parents must have rules and expectations for their teen's choices and behaviors. Even so, it will be important for parents to avoid the tendency simply to say no because they feel uncomfortable with their teen's request. Smart, faithful parents will make liberal use of the qualified-yes technique that we discussed in chapter 4. For instance, it is one thing to say to your teen, "I notice that when I let you hang out with Mike, your language goes in the gutter. In order to know that you are mature enough to be around him, I need to see you not just controlling your language in general, but encouraging your brothers and sisters to speak respectfully around the house. If I can see you demonstrating that kind of maturity and leadership, I can let you hang around Mike more often. It's up to you." It is another thing to say to your teen, "Mike's a bad influence on you. I don't want you hanging around that kid."

Again, if teens see the faith as exclusionary or as a complication to their relationships, they will tend to reject it as "bad." On the other hand if they see an obvious personal or relational benefit to following the rules and morals of their faith, they will tend to own those teachings and defend them even when it costs them dearly to do so.

3. *Find positive outside-family support.* Giving your teen the opportunity to build relationships with peers who take their faith seriously can be a tremendous blessing. That said, parents often make the mistake of thinking that a youth group or another positive faith-based group outside the family can make up for the lack of a strong faith-based family life. This is not the case. In the absence of a positive, faith-based family relationship and a discipline style that helps rather than hinders your child's ability to meet his goals, your child will either not be amenable to or will absolutely resist any benefit he could get from joining a youth group or going on a high school retreat. Likewise, if your teen isn't able to find faithful, engaged peers in your neighborhood, it might be lonely for your teen, but it won't be the end of the world if he can still see you as his primary support because of the attachment and positive discipleship he experiences in his relationship with you.

Even realizing that a good faith-based peer group can't really substitute for a strong faith-based family life, it can be a tremendous support to your teen. When a teen experiences a strong, faith-based family life and is able to find a strong faith-based peer group to support him, it creates a synergy that is extremely beneficial and can propel your child to a much deeper and stronger personal sense of faith.

Research also shows that giving your kids an opportunity to build relationships with other adults who have a strong faith and can serve as supportive mentors or examples can be tremendously helpful (Smith, 2014). The best way to do this naturally is by cultivating friendships with other families who share your passion for the faith and by becoming involved as a family in the life of your parish (see chapter 16 for more ideas on this).

The takeway from this point is that although other relationships with faithful peers or adult mentors can be tremendously helpful, they cannot serve as a replacement or substitute for your family. The Church reminds parents that we are our children's "primary educators" when it comes to forming their faith and character. Our parish, Catholic school, youth group, and other people affiliated with our faith community can serve significant and important supportive roles, but we can't rely on these people and organizations to do our work for us.

4. *Give teens a faith-based cause to fight for.* Because people at the Relationship-Based Faith Stage see the goodness of faith in terms of its ability to increase people's ability to connect, it can be important to encourage your teen's involvement in various social-justice issues, such as fighting for the rights of the unborn, antipoverty initiatives, charitable works, and other forms of positive Christian social activism. Developmentally, teens are searching for their identity. Having an important social cause to fight for can be an important identity-building tool for adolescents, and seeing that this cause is related to the faith helps teens place faith-based activism at the heart of their identity development.

In a later chapter, we'll discuss how to facilitate your child's sense of mission, but we include it here because adolescence is really the time when concerns about mission and social action are key to faith development.

The more teens are able to encounter faith as an effective instrument for helping them find their place in the world, both in terms of finding a community to belong to and a mission to serve, the more they will be prepared to enter into an adult experience of faith.

Faith Stages 5 through 7

Because stages 5 through 7 are adult stages of faith, we will not belabor them here. But we do wish to mention them as a way of helping you understand the stages of faith that lie ahead and the basic challenges one must overcome to work through these stages.

Stage 5 is *Personal Faith* (what Fowler calls the Individuative-Reflective Stage). At this stage, the person has cultivated a relatively deep and personally meaningful prayer life, found some kind of community to support his faith development, and developed a strong personal sense of mission. This is the first stage that represents a mature, adult faith. Experts estimate that only about 2 percent of Catholic adults are at this stage (Weddell, 2015). (Note: That is a depressing number and needs to be much higher, but statistically speaking, considering that the Church claims 1.3 billion members worldwide, this percentage represents about 26 million Catholics around the globe.)

The person at the Personal Faith Stage focuses his attention on the question: How must my faith change *me* on a deeper level? To some degree, every stage is concerned with some dimension of personal growth and change, but this stage in particular is concerned with asking and resolving hard questions about one's personal experience of faith, seeking how he must change in order to be a better example of his faith and how he must live out his faith more fully in all his relationships. It is a faith stage characterized by the call to *metanoia*, a call of the Holy Spirit to deeper, internal, personal conversion marked by the desire to address deeper questions about how one's faith applies to him, combined with a humility that allows the person to admit that he doesn't know all the answers and that he must willingly seek help and guidance to deepen his spiritual journey.

Stage 6 is *Integrated Faith* (or as Fowler calls it, Conjunctive Faith). At this stage the believer seeks to leave behind any remaining desire to cling to his comfort zone with regard to faith and religion. Various religious practices (the Rosary, chaplets, novenas, adoration, prayer forms) that were previously ignored or looked down on are given a second look, and various teachings that were previously rejected or sidelined are reexamined with an eye toward discovering previously underappreciated treasures. Paradoxes, such as how to be both doctrinally sound and pastorally sensitive, or how to be courageously truthful yet authentically loving, are explored and mastered at this stage as the person seeks to integrate the remaining aspects of his faith life that couldn't be made to fit before. This stage is most consistent with what spiritual directors refer to as the Illuminative Way — the stage of spiritual maturity marked by both wisdom and zeal for doing the Lord's work.

Stage 7 is *Universalizing Faith* (the same in Fowler). At this stage, the person is perfectly integrated into his faith tradition but also capable of being extraordinarily generous to the truths that may be found in the faith traditions of others. This isn't the "go along to get along" syncretism that often typifies the

Relationship-Based Faith Stage. Rather, it is a much more intentional, mindful, generous, and authentic approach to ongoing faith development whereupon the individual is fully committed to, rooted in, and firmly believing in his faith tradition while open to the ways God might still be reaching out to him and others through different and competing faith traditions. Examples may include Pope St. John Paul the Great's actions in Assisi at the World Day of Prayer, St. Teresa of Calcutta's generosity toward the faith life of her Hindu neighbors, or Pope Francis's visit to a Buddhist temple in Sri Lanka to demonstrate his "friendship and positive attitude" toward Buddhists. All these individuals were able to see the goodness and beauty in other religious traditions without having to go so far as to say that these other traditions were equal to Catholicism.

This stage might most closely be associated with what spiritual directors refer to as the late Illuminative Way or even the early Unitive Way, the latter being the stage of spiritual maturity at which one has achieved a degree of union with God even before death — in other words, a living saint.

Conclusion

We hope that through this brief guide to the stages of faith, you were able to get a sense of your own faith journey as well as your children's, and you will be better prepared to meet the needs that will enable you and yours to proceed to the next level of conversion and intimacy with God. Obviously, this has not been meant to be anything but the briefest overview of Fowler's stages of faith, nor does it intend to be a completely comprehensive guide to meeting the needs and overcoming the challenges of each stage. Nevertheless, by understanding how our basic human need to make meaning and seek significance evolves over the stages of the human life cycle, you can understand the work that God wants to do in your own life and in your children's so you can participate more effectively in that work and allow God to take your family's faith to a new and more intimate, meaningful level.

Part 2

Discovering God Together:
Celebrating a Life of Faith

6

The Family That Prays Together: A How-To

The family that prays together stays together.

—Servant of God Fr. Patrick Peyton, C.S.C.

As we mentioned earlier, St. Jean Vianney said that "prayer is nothing less than union with God." In other words, prayer is about intimacy. It is about building relationship with God and the people we pray with. Prayer is also the means by which God teaches us to have the kinds of relationships he wants to give us—relationships rooted in his love. When we sit at the feet of the Author of Love, he instructs our hearts on how to live his vision of family life. This is more than a pious sentiment. It is the lived experience of families who have an authentic family prayer life.

What can families who pray together—not in a perfunctory way but in a heartfelt manner—expect to learn about how God wants them to love each other? In his Theology of the Body (2006), Pope St. John Paul the Great reminds us that God's love is *free*, *total*, *faithful*, and *fruitful*.

- *Free*. God calls families who pray together to love each other freely—willingly and cheerfully (as opposed to grudgingly and under pressure) —and to look for ways to make each other's lives easier and more pleasant.

• *Total.* God will teach families who cultivate an authentic, heartfelt prayer life to love each other totally; not to hold back but to share openly, to seek help willingly, and to trust each other completely.

• *Faithful.* Families who pray together will receive the grace to love each other faithfully. They will learn to be able to count on each other, not to be afraid to trust each other, to know that they will always be there for each other—not just in a symbolic way—but in a real, tangible, emotional way.

• *Fruitful.* Families who pray together will discover the mission that God called them together to serve—a mission that enables them to live meaningful lives, work for the good of their community, and build the Kingdom of God.

Of course, for many parents who are new to family prayer, the biggest question is not "How can I create a prayer life that serves as the heart of the intimacy of my family life and our relationship with God?" but rather, "How can I get my kids to sit still long enough to do it?" If you identified with the latter question—even to a small degree—then fear not. The following pages will take you, step by step, through how you can create an experience of family prayer that is truly soul satisfying.

This chapter offers a template that you can follow while you are finding your own spiritual feet or a point of reference you can use to see how you might further develop your family's spiritual life.

The Family That Prays Together: A How-To

The prayers in this chapter — indeed, all the ideas in this book — are not checklist items. Rather, they are opportunities to invite God into your home so that he can teach you to love him, each other, and everyone you meet throughout the day, with the free, total, faithful, and fruitful love that comes from his heart.

Family Prayer: A Rule of Life

In religious communities (e.g., Franciscans, Benedictines, Jesuits, Dominicans), the whole community of sisters, brothers, or priests gathers together at various points throughout the day to pray together. These regular prayer times make up an important part of what is called the community's rule of life — that is, the rituals and routines they practice so that they can learn to join together in the love and service of God, each other, and the world.

Although family life is very different from life in a religious community, any family that really wants both to enjoy the closeness that we've described throughout this book and to be a sign to the world of God's love is also called to create a kind of rule of life that will be unique to them. The Catholic family, as a domestic church, must also come together to pray throughout the day so that they too can more effectively learn to love and serve God, each other, and the people they meet throughout the day. As parents and children work to discover God together, prayer, rather than being an afterthought, becomes the engine that drives the love and relationships within the home. This is the kind of prayer life we wish for your family.

As you read the following suggestions for building a meaningful family prayer life, we ask you to offer a prayer from your heart that God would draw you and yours closer to him and to each other.

Lord Jesus Christ, let our family dedicate our hearts to you. Help us to love you and each other in a way that fills our hearts with the fire of your love. Inspired by the example of your Holy Family, help each one of us, parents and children, make a sincere gift of ourselves to each other throughout the day so that in all our interactions with each other we can cultivate "a respect for others, a sense of justice, cordial openness, dialogue, generous service, solidarity and all the other values which help us live our life as a gift." We ask this through the intercession of the Holy Family and in the name of Jesus Christ, our Lord and Brother.

Morning Offering

Mornings are a crazy-busy time for families. There is so much to do to get ready for work and school. Most families are lucky if they can get out the door each morning without killing each other, and we have certainly experienced that ourselves. But if we're going to live the Catholic difference authentically in our family and personal lives, it is important to take even some brief time to pray together at the start of the day. It requires only a few minutes, but it can make all the difference in the world.

The Church encourages all the faithful to pray a "morning offering," a brief prayer that calls the day to mind and asks God to help us gracefully approach the tasks and challenges ahead. Here is an example of how we've adapted this idea for our family. Feel free to use it or change it so that it works for your family.

When you wake your kids, take a minute to call everyone together to snuggle in bed. Collect the family together so that you begin the day with a brief reminder that you are all there for each other and that you don't have to face the day on your own. Give everyone their morning hugs and kisses, and then take a moment to dedicate your day as a family to God. Here is an example of a prayer you could say, but the spirit of the prayer is more important than the words. Use your own words and adapt the following prayer so that it reflects the intentions of your family.

In the Name of the Father, the Son, and the Holy Spirit. Amen.

Dear Jesus, we give you our family and the day ahead. Help us to be here for each other and, because of our love for each other and your presence in our lives, never to feel alone at any point in the day. Lord, we give you every word we say, every thought we think, and everything we do, and we ask you to bless us so that we can give glory to you in everything and that our family can be a blessing to each other and a light to the world.

Next, ask if anyone has any special intentions to pray for. Take turns expressing those intentions out loud. Then finish with: "We ask all of this in the Name of the Father, and of the Son, and of the Holy Spirit. Amen."

Again, feel free to do your own version of a family morning offering using your own words, but keep it short and sweet. In the busy, crazy time of most mornings in families, less really is more when it comes to your morning offering. But taking even a few minutes to gather your family together and remind each other of the importance of being there for each other and living each day for God can help you start the day on the right foot and remind you that every moment of every day is bursting with grace and heavenly purpose.

Discovering God Together

Giving Your Children Blessings and Praying Over Them

Another wonderful idea for creating a meaningful family prayer life is to pray over your children. We are in the habit of praying over our children before they go to school, games, or performances, each evening after nighttime family prayers, and when they are in special need of grace (e.g., if they are injured, or struggling, or sad).

This is another simple activity that takes only a few seconds but can go a long way toward making family prayer personal and meaningful. Saying brief prayers over your children is a way to ask God to be with your children throughout their day when you can't be, to oversee their overall growth in wisdom and grace, and to be there in special times when they need a little extra hug from God. Praying over your children is another simple way to invite God into the little moments of your everyday life.

The key is to keep these prayers brief and personal. There are no formulas, and you should definitely use your own words. Begin by placing your hand on your child's head or shoulder; we believe the physical contact is an important part of making this prayer of blessing meaningful, personal, and intimate. Then bring your intentions for your child before the Lord. Here are some examples of the kinds of prayers we say over our children every day.

Before school or performances: *Lord, bless N. Give him peace of mind and heart. Help him to use his gifts and talents to give you glory in everything he does. Give him a wonderful day [or experience], help him know how much you love him, and let him love you first and most. Amen.*

For a special intention: *Lord, please bless N. Heal him [calm his nerves, give him wisdom, et cetera] and help him* to know that you are right here, loving him and comforting him with your Holy Spirit. Fill him with your grace and peace, and let him know how precious he is to you and to us. Amen.

At night: Lord, thank you for this wonderful child. Bless him. Help him to know what a gift he is to this family and to the world. Give him a good night's sleep, and help him wake up ready to bless you. Give him a long, joyful, prosperous, healthy life, filled with people who love him and whom he can love. Help him to discover all the gifts and talents you've given him and use those gifts to be a blessing to others and to give you glory. Above all, let him love you with all his heart, mind, soul, and strength all the days of his life, and love others as you love him. Amen.

These are just some examples. Feel free to use your own words. The point is to bring God into the little moments of everyday life with your child and to make God your partner in parenting your child by bringing his joy to bear on times your child is happy, his consolation when your child is sad, his grace when your child needs help, and his counsel when you and your child need a little wisdom.

Grace at Meals

Many families offer some kind of grace at meals, but you can get more out this time by personalizing it in addition to using the traditional mealtime prayers. Use mealtime prayers — especially Grace at dinner — as a special time to give thanks to God for the little blessings that have occurred since the last time you spoke with him. That could be as simple as thanking him for helping you all get ready in time for breakfast or, if you haven't seen each other since your morning prayer, thanking him for the little ways he has made his presence felt in your lives throughout the day.

Begin by making the Sign of the Cross—an important prayer itself that indicates that you are a son or daughter of God and a disciple of Jesus Christ. Then say something like this: "God, we thank you for giving us this time to be together. We thank you for …" and let everyone at the table offer a few words of thanks. Then you can wrap things up with traditional Grace before Meals:

And finally, we ask you to [all together] bless us, O Lord, and these thy gifts, which we are about to receive from thy bounty. Through Christ our Lord. Amen.

Saying Grace at meals reminds us that God is the source of every good thing in our lives and gives us a moment to express our gratitude for even the little things he does. We encourage you to take a moment to say Grace as a family even when you are eating at a restaurant or at a friend's house. You can be discreet. Praying isn't about putting on a show. But it is important to give God thanks wherever we are, and acknowledging God publicly for the many gifts he gives us is not only an important part of our devotion to God; it is also a powerful way to remind others to take a moment to thank God for the blessings they have received. Remember, God wants to change the world through your family. Give him the chance to bless others through your simple witness, not because you are trying to show off, but because you are remembering to thank God, together, in humility and love.

Aspirations

Aspirations are simple expressions of gratitude or requests for help that we make throughout the day. "Lord, thank you for finding me this great parking space." "God, please help me find my keys!" "Lord Jesus, please bless Jennifer. Help her with her presentation." Aspirations are simple ways we keep God at our side throughout the day.

In addition to modeling these simple prayers of gratitude and supplication (the technical word for "asking God for help"), we should prompt our children to make these simple exclamations as well. After we have kissed that scraped knee and are applying the bandage, we can say, "Why don't we ask Jesus to help heal that boo-boo?" Then either you can say, "Jesus, please heal Mary's boo-boo" or have your child say it if she is willing. When your child brings you a drawing or plays his lesson well, after you have praised him sincerely and given him a hug, suggest, "Let's take a minute to thank God for giving you such wonderful talents!" Then you can say, "Thank you, Jesus, for giving Alex the ability to draw [or play the piano] so well." Or, you can have your child say it if he is willing.

Likewise, remind your children to talk to God throughout the day when they are at school, at the game, or with their friends, because God loves them so much and wants to be part of every moment of their lives.

Aspirations are lovely, simple, and personal ways to remind us that God is always right by our side, working for our good, helping us through struggles, and blessing us in little ways. They can be a truly important part of helping our children develop an up-close-and-personal relationship with Jesus Christ.

Family Prayer Time

In our chapter on rituals and routines, we spoke of the importance of a more formal, daily prayer time. Families are often intimidated by this idea. "What do we say?" "How do we get the kids to be still for it?" As with other ways of praying together as a family, keeping it short, personal, meaningful, and intimate is the best way to help children be attentive and involved.

Some families like to kneel beside the bed for family prayer. This is a great way to use our whole bodies to enter into the experience of prayer. Even so, it's okay—and even admirable—to sit with your children on your lap or have them next to you with your arms around them during prayer time. Especially with smaller children in the Feeling-Based/Intuitive-Projective Stage, making prayer time a time of close family affection enables God to convey his love for your children through you. Plus, keeping little ones on your lap is a good way to make sure no one gets a bad case of the wiggles. There is no one right posture for family prayer. Do whatever works best to communicate that this is a serious but loving and intimate time as a family.

There are many ways to pray as a family. As Catholics, you should feel free to explore the Church's spiritual treasure chest, which contains thousands of years of wonderful traditions, devotions, and prayer forms.

We have found it best to have a loose template to follow using the acronym PRAISE.

P   Praise and thanksgiving
R   Repentance
A   Ask for your needs
I   Intercede for others
S   Seek God's will
E   Express your desire to serve him until you meet again in prayer

The nice thing about this format is that, depending on your energy level and attention span, it could take five minutes or an hour. You could add formal prayers (such as the Our Father, the Hail Mary, the Glory Be, the Memorare, the St. Michael Prayer, the Rosary, or the Divine Mercy Chaplet) at the beginning or the end if you like, or you can keep it more spontaneous if that works better for your family.

When using this template, the leader of the prayer should start. When children are younger, Dad or Mom should lead, but as children get older—say, around six or seven—they can take turns leading, assuming they are willing and have enough experience praying with the family to know how to do it well (more on this in the next chapter). Decide ahead of time whether you are going to use just this format or add any other prayers that your family finds meaningful; then go through each step, with each family member making a brief contribution. You don't have to do each step every time. This outline just helps you remember to incorporate different dimensions of prayer into your family prayer time.

> *Praise and thanksgiving.* Praise is when we honor God for who he is, like saying to a person we love, "You're so awesome! I'm so glad you're in my life!" Thanksgiving is when we honor God for the things he has done for us. Let each family member, beginning with the leader, offer a brief word of praise or thanks. Don't force a reluctant or shy child to say something, but do encourage him. You might say, "Jimmy, would it be okay for me to thank God that you had fun playing a game with me today?" (Nod.) "Jesus, Jimmy is *so thankful* that we got to play a game together! Thank you, Jesus!" (Little hug for Jimmy.) Be encouraging and gentle. Everyone will participate eventually.

Repentance. This isn't time for confessing personal sins. That's what Confession is for! But almost every day in family life we have little ways we take advantage of each other or hurt each other's feelings. This is a good time to acknowledge those little lapses and ask for God's help to do better. For instance, "Lord, I'm sorry for losing patience with the kids. Help me to be more patient while getting everyone out the door in the morning." Then you might ask the children, "How about you? Is there some way you'd like God to help you be more loving to the family?" Again, don't pressure. Encourage, prompt, and suggest when necessary, but be gentle and be careful not to embarrass anyone.

Ask for your needs. We're all pretty good at this. Take turns bringing various concerns and needs to God. "Lord, please help me get along better with the people at work." "God, please help me do well on my math test tomorrow." And so forth.

Intercede for others. Remember to let everyone take turns praying for those who need God's grace. "Lord, please bless Grandma and help her feel better."

Seek God's will. This is similar to asking for your needs, but it has more to do with bigger decisions that require some ongoing thought and discussion. For instance, "Lord, we really want to be closer as a family, but it's so hard to find the time. Help us decide which activities are really important and which ones we could let go of so we could have more family time." Or, "Lord, help us all work well together in deciding which college would be best for

Emily. She has worked so hard and you've given her so many wonderful opportunities. Please help her make the right decision and help us be a good support to her." You should also use this time to talk a little bit about any new information you've gotten since the last time you prayed about this issue or any new questions that have come up. This gives you the chance to remember to make God a part of the most important discussions and decisions your family has to make.

Express your desire to serve him until you meet again in prayer. Family prayer doesn't end when you say, "Amen." In some ways, it is just beginning. If you let him, God will continue speaking to you all throughout the day by bringing something to mind or highlighting something someone says to you, or drawing your attention to something that he wants you to think about some more. As you wrap up your family prayer time, end by letting God know that you want to listen to him all day long and bring what he tells you back to your next family prayer time. "Lord, thank you for this time together. Help us to keep listening to you, hearing your voice, and attending to your will throughout the day until we meet again as a family to pray and honor you. Amen."

Again, these are just suggestions. You can add or subtract anything you like. If you would like to add a praise song, go ahead. If you want to add a decade of the Rosary, by all means, do so. If you need to keep it shorter tonight because you got home late from a game, that's okay too. Just make a regular commitment to some kind of daily family prayer time so that your family can acknowledge all the ways God is active in your hearts and in your home.

Discovering God Together

The Rosary

When Servant of God Fr. Patrick Peyton said, "The family that prays together stays together," he was thinking of the Rosary specifically. Even so, praying a family Rosary well can be a challenge.

When you pray a family Rosary, the point is not just to get through it at the speed of light so you can finish before all the kids wander off. The point is to give you a way to think about the life of Jesus. The Rosary is supposed to be a simple way to learn meditative prayer. Meditative prayer is a more mature form of prayer. Think of it this way: Which is a more intimate conversation—to remind your spouse to pick up the dry cleaning or to think and talk about all the things you've been through together? Obviously the latter is the more meaningful conversation. That's what meditation is. Instead of just telling God what happened today or what you need, meditation gives you a chance to reflect on the life of Jesus—all the things he did and went through—and what that means to you today.

There are four sets of mysteries (traditionally there were three, but Pope St. John Paul the Great added the Luminous Mysteries in 2002). The Joyful Mysteries (usually prayed on Mondays and Saturdays) are the Annunciation, the Visitation (of Mary to Elizabeth, who was pregnant with John the Baptist), the Nativity, the Presentation of Jesus in the Temple, and the Finding of Jesus in the Temple.

The Luminous Mysteries (usually prayed on Thursdays) look at Jesus' ministry: the Baptism of the Lord, the Wedding Feast at Cana, the Proclamation of the Kingdom, the Transfiguration, and the Institution of the Eucharist.

The Sorrowful Mysteries (usually prayed on Tuesdays and Fridays) are the Agony in the Garden, the Scourging at the

Pillar, the Crowning with Thorns, the Carrying of the Cross, and the Crucifixion.

The Glorious Mysteries (usually prayed on Sundays and Wednesdays) are the Resurrection of Jesus, the Ascension of Jesus, the Descent of the Holy Spirit on Pentecost, the Assumption of Mary, and the Crowning of Mary as Queen of heaven and earth.

As you see, praying the Rosary gives us a chance to recall the entire life of Christ each week and reflect on how our lives can more closely mirror Christ's. That said, in praying the Rosary as a family, it is best to start small. Although it is obviously ideal to work up to praying the entire Rosary, it is perfectly acceptable to limit yourselves to praying a single decade of the Rosary and focus on a specific instance of Christ's life.

Whether you choose to pray one decade of the Rosary or the set of mysteries for that given day, begin by reminding your children what the decade is about and ask them how they think Jesus (or one of the other people in the mystery — e.g., Mary, Elizabeth, John the Baptist, Simeon and Anna) felt. Ask them if they have ever felt that way. Ask them to think about all this as they say the Our Father, the ten Hail Marys, and the Glory Be that make up a decade of the Rosary. The point is to make it personal and meaningful, not to charge through it like a locomotive running behind schedule. To do so is, as Pope Paul VI observed, almost worse than not praying at all and completely in defiance of Jesus' command to avoid the "vain repetition of words."

The family Rosary is a wonderful way to teach your children how to begin to meditate on the life of Christ and how we might conform our lives more closely to his. Obviously, praying the Rosary with the right focus and spirit takes some time and practice. Be patient. Be gentle. And be respectful of your limits and those of your children. As with all things, challenge them to do their best, but don't push them so hard that they lose heart or lose interest in the prayer. Do what you can, and let the Holy Spirit do the rest.

There are many sources online to walk you step by step through the mechanics of praying the Rosary. Holy Cross Family Ministries (HCFM.org, founded by Fr. Patrick Peyton) is committed to helping families learn to pray together in general and to pray the family Rosary in particular. A great book on this topic and on the topic of prayer in general is *The How-To Book of Catholic Devotions* by Regis Flaherty and Mike Aquilina.

Other Formal Prayers

There are so many ways to pray as a family. The Church has many rich prayer traditions, and you should feel free to learn as many of them as you can. Spontaneous prayers from the heart are beautiful, but using formal prayers — the prayers that have drawn our brothers and sisters in faith closer to the Lord for centuries — helps to join our hearts and minds to the heart of the Church. Whether we are talking about a simple Our Father, the Rosary, a chaplet, a novena, a consecration, or another devotion, each formal prayer has been tested through the experience of thousands — if not millions — of people and found to be an effective means of drawing us closer to the heart of God.

The aforementioned *How-To Book of Catholic Devotions* by Regis Flaherty and Mike Aquilina is a wonderful resource, as is the U.S. Conference of Catholic Bishops' *Catholic Household Blessings and Prayers*. This latter book includes prayers over your Advent Wreath, Christmas tree, and Nativity set and prayers for the first day of school, for anniversaries, for birthdays, and for a host of other feasts and family occasions. It is a treasure for any family that wants to discover God together and cultivate a closer relationship with him. We use it a great deal, especially around holidays.

Filled with the Spirit

This chapter has provided only a glimpse of the myriad ways you can pray as a family. We never intended to write a comprehensive volume of family prayer. But we hope that this chapter will help make the idea of family prayer more attractive and doable for your family. We hope that our suggestions will make family prayer a more meaningful experience that fuels the fires of love in your home by filling your hearts with the Holy Spirit, who will guide you in living out an uncommonly close family life that nurtures your soul and gives witness to the world of God's plan for all families.

7

Developing Your Children's Prayer Lives

It's one thing to pray as a family, but it's another thing to raise
prayerful kids. Many parents are surprised by this distinction.
They think that if their children are raised around prayer, it will
automatically sink in. The fact that only 33 percent of children
raised in homes where both parents regularly go to church attend church regularly as adults should be a sobering reality check
(Haug and Warner, 2000). Although there is no question that
attending Mass and praying as a family is critical to forming
faithful children, there is obviously something more required to
make children own their faith into adulthood.

Many Catholic parents come to assume that it is only natural for children to fall away from the faith for a time (usually around college age) and then make their way back to the
Church sometime after they have children of their own. To
our way of thinking, this was never really a good thing—as
it implies a more ritualistic than a personal connection to
faith—but even if you have felt more optimistically about
this finding, it is becoming less and less possible to count on
this adult return to the Church, especially as more and more
children are being raised in divorced and single-parent households in which all traditions and rituals—especially religious

ones — tend to be less stable and frequent and thus have less power to impact adult behavior.

More than ever, it is important to set our children's hearts on fire with the love of God from an early age and to foster their personal relationship with Jesus Christ so that, rather than riding on our coattails, they can have their own, up-close-and-personal encounter with God that will sustain them.

Invite Your Child to Lead Your Family Prayer

Children need to begin their personal prayer life by learning to pray with Mom or Dad first. Creating some kind of family prayer ritual is critical for raising prayerful children. Your child's prayer life is the fruit of the seeds planted by your example of personal prayer and the experience of regular, meaningful family prayer.

You can begin transitioning your child to a personal prayer life by slowly and gently encouraging him to lead family prayer. As your child demonstrates the ability to contribute consistently to family prayer, float the idea. "Do you think you would like to lead family prayer tomorrow?" If your child is nervous about the idea, let him know you will be there to coach him through the steps. If your child still seems nervous, just say, "Well, it will be important for you to be able to lead family prayer someday, but it's okay if that's not today or tomorrow. I'm just really proud of how you contribute to family prayer, and I think you can lead it whenever you're ready." Don't hound your child, but mention the possibility again every few weeks. In time, your child will be eager to take on this role.

When your child does agree to lead, be a gentle coach. Remind him of the steps of whatever format you usually use — whether it is formal prayer, or the PRAISE template, or something of your own design. Let your child sit close to you and put your arm around him so that he can feel your presence, love, and support. Then just be casual about it. Other than reminding your child of the steps if he gets stuck, let him lead as he chooses and say whatever he feels led to say.

When your child has finished leading a particular section, ask him to invite others in the family to offer their thanks or intentions. When prayer time is over, be sure to thank your child for doing such a great job leading. Let him know how proud you are that he has taken these first steps toward owning his faith and how proud God is that he is showing such maturity in his prayer life.

Teach Your Child to Be a Blessing

In the last chapter, we talked about praying over your children and giving them blessings. As your children grow, it is important to let them learn how to pray over you and give you blessings too. God wants to use all his children, no matter how small, to be a blessing in the world.

When we give our children the opportunity to pray over us and lead prayer in the home, we teach them that they can make a difference and that God wants to use them to bring his grace into the world. They need to understand that all the grace they are given is a gift to be used. The more they learn that they can use their spiritual gifts, the more they will come to own them.

Individual Prayer Time: Why?

Building on the importance of teaching children to use their spiritual gifts, research by University of Notre Dame sociologist Christian Smith found that even children who are raised by two highly religious parents will not necessarily go on to be faithful adults unless they are also taught how to make a personal connection with their faith and spiritual gifts (2014).

Author Sherry Weddell refers to the process of teaching people how to use their spiritual gifts as "forming intentional disciples" (2012). Children too, must be taught to be intentional disciples. Although the phrase "intentional disciple" is new, the concept isn't. To have any healthy relationships, children need to be taught to be intentional about their relationships. That's why, although family prayer is essential for raising faithful children, it isn't enough on its own. We need to teach our children how to experience God for themselves. Here are some suggestions for getting started.

Individual Prayer Times
for Kids: A How-To

Start with the familiar. Once your children are used to family prayer and have begun to lead family prayer reasonably well themselves (usually by at least age six, if not sooner), it's time to help your children learn to pray on their own. Start with what they are familiar with — that is, use your family prayer format as the basic outline for your children's individual prayer time.

Make a space. Explain to your child that he is old enough and has shown such maturity in leading family prayer that it's time to learn to talk to God on his own as well. To celebrate this milestone, it can be a fun ritual to create a prayer space together with your child. In a corner of your child's room, set up a small, kid-size table and chair (an inexpensive plastic set from the dollar store will do). Cover the table with some attractive material scraps, or have your child decorate an inexpensive pillowcase by drawing pictures of his favorite Bible stories or even Scripture quotes and use that to cover the table. Let your child choose a small, child-friendly statue of Jesus at a religious-goods store and a statue, picture, or prayer card of his favorite or patron saint. Add a good Catholic children's Bible to the mix. Explain that although God is with your child always and everywhere he goes, this will be his special prayer-time corner where he can have his own visits with Jesus each evening before family prayer.

Make time. Each evening, set aside a few minutes for individual prayer time before family prayer time. At first, five minutes will be more than enough, but as your child gets older, he will most likely ask for more time.

Coach your child. During the first few times, stay with your child and coach him through individual prayer. Have him read a Bible story of his choice. Ask him to think about what it felt like to be the characters in the story. Ask him if he has ever felt like the people in the story. Next, teach him to conclude his spiritual-reading time by asking Jesus to open his heart and mind so that God can teach him to love him with all his heart, mind, soul, and strength. You can even have your child end this part of prayer by saying, "I love you, Jesus! In the Name of the Father, and of the Son and of the Holy Spirit."

In the beginning, this might be enough. When your child seems ready for more, you might adapt the PRAISE format for individual use. Walk your child through the steps, but ask him to try to be a little more personal with each point, talking to God about things he might not have time to share in family prayer.

Collect your child. Make a bridge from individual prayer time to family prayer. Call your children together, and ask each child to share one thing that he thought about during his individual prayer time. What was one thing about the Bible story he read or the thoughts he had as he imagined being the characters in the story or even as he prayed afterward. You and your spouse should offer simple reflections from your own prayer time or from what you were thinking as you helped the younger children pray. Once each person has shared a thought or reflection from his individual prayer time, move into the steps of your family prayer time.

Be flexible. As your child becomes more comfortable with whatever format you have suggested to him (as evidenced by the quality of his sharing at family prayer time) give him new opportunities to pray in new ways. You might try a more mature translation of the Bible. Or get him his own rosary and teach him how to pray at least a decade thoughtfully. Ask your pastor or parish director of religious education (DRE) for other ideas that can develop your child's prayer life.

This whole approach from the beginning of your children's individual prayer time to the conclusion of your family prayer time might take ten to fifteen minutes at first and might extend to thirty minutes as your children get older and more familiar with the process. You should certainly feel free to adapt it to your needs. The only "right way" to pray is the way that leads your children to a closer relationship with God and with each other.

The beauty of this approach to family prayer is that it serves as an opportunity for family bonding. It fosters a discipleship relationship between you and your child and helps you learn how to be your child's de facto spiritual director, which is not only appropriate, but desirable at this stage of the game.

Can I Get a Witness? The Importance of "God Talk"

Another important dimension of raising prayerful kids is giving them a witness of how God is an active part of your everyday life and experience and the everyday life and experience of the people you know and admire. Research indicates that what we call "God talk," that is, sharing stories about the ways God has been present in your daily life in terms of the times you feel close to him or cared for by him, or the times you or those you know have been helped by him in both natural and miraculous ways, is a truly important part of giving your children an active faith and personal prayer life (Smith, 2014).

Christians often speak of the importance of "witnessing" the faith to others — that is, sharing stories about the powerful ways God has impacted and continues to impact your life and the lives of those you know. Without these stories, faith can too easily become an intellectual exercise or a dry, meaningless habit. God is alive and active! He wants his presence to be felt. He desires to be known in real and tangible ways. When we talk at the dinner table about how God blessed us that day, or share experiences of answered prayer, and marvel at the ways God has impacted the lives of those we love in positive ways, our children learn that they can expect God not just to hear their prayers but to respond to them and answer them. These stories fuel our children's desire to pray by teaching them to have an expectant faith (see Mark 11:23) — that is, a faith in a God who is alive and active and who desires to have a positive, powerful, and deeply felt influence on the activities of our daily lives.

Conclusion

As with the other recommendations in this book, this chapter is not meant to be viewed as "the one right way" to teach your children to pray on their own, nor is it meant to be a compre-hensive guide to fostering your child's prayer life. We hope that these past few chapters have given you a clearer sense of how prayer and family prayer can truly serve as the heart of intimacy in your home, where you and your children can learn to live life as a gift in the family "school of love" at the feet of the Author of Love himself.

8

Family: On a Mission from God

Your family and your children are on a mission from God. As we've shared throughout this book, God wants to use your family to transform the world! Don't worry; you don't have to be perfect in order for God to accomplish this mission in your life. You just have to (1) commit to living out the Catholic vision of family life regardless of the challenges you face within your family or in the world; (2) work to cultivate an active family and personal prayer life; and (3) discover your family's mission.

We explored the first two of these three points earlier in the book. Now, let's look at what it means to cultivate your family mission.

Discerning Your Family Charism

Every religious community has a particular mission or charism it is known for: preaching, ministering to the poor, providing healthcare, and so on—that is, the specific way the religious community believes it has been called to witness to God's love in the world.

You might be surprised to discover that your family has a mission or charism too! Just as there are Cistercians and Benedictines and Paulists and Marists, and each of these orders (and every other order) has been called to bear witness to God's love in the world in a unique way, so the Smiths and the Joneses and the Popcaks and your family are each a kind of religious community (i.e., a domestic church) that God has called together to bear witness to an unique dimension of his life and love in the world. You live out your family's charism in two ways:

1. You live out your charism as a Catholic family simply by trying your best each day to live out the Catholic vision of family life prayerfully, by being a family rooted in the free, total, faithful, and fruitful love that springs from God's heart, and by creating an atmosphere that exemplifies a "respect for others, a sense of justice, cordial openness, dialogue, generous service, solidarity and all the other values which help people to live life as a gift."

2. You can take this mission to a new level by prayerfully discovering and celebrating the unique gifts and qualities God has established in your family, such as hospitality, service, education, or health.

A charism is simply a talent or interest that your family has that you decide, together, to place in service to God in some way. For example, a family we know celebrates the charism of hospitality by hosting small get-togethers and parties for saints' days and other feasts. Their Epiphany party, along with games and special foods, is legendary. Another family we know that has a charism of health and fitness, and they have dedicated their gift to God by making sure that their children and the teams they coach practice good sportsmanship on the field. We know a family of musicians who use their charism by volunteering to play for various charitable benefits and community events. Yet another family loves to garden, and they bring some of their best produce and flowers to the nursing home, to shut-ins, or to the local food bank and soup kitchen.

Finally, in our own family, we have a gift for public speaking and teaching. Our children work with us in our ministry and when we speak at conferences. In fact, part of our agreement as a family is that we don't accept any speaking engagement that doesn't enable us to travel as a family. We believe very strongly that God has called us not only to preach "family first" but to live it. When they were younger, our kids helped us manage our booth and distribute literature. As they got older, they started accepting speaking engagements at various youth events and other events as well. The experiences we've had on the road and interacting with families all over the world has been a source of some wonderful family moments and great opportunities to serve God together.

Discovering your charism often involves looking at the most meaningful activity in your family's rituals and routines and then finding simple ways to devote that activity or gift to God. Your family charism will become the way God shows his love to the world through the gifts he has shared with you and your children. It can become a terrific way your family can be a blessing to the world and convey a sense of mission to your children.

In our chapter on the stages of faith we referenced research stating that children are much more likely to be personally faithful as adults when they are given a faithful cause to serve in the preteen and teen years. Your family charism can be a big part of that mission. One recent study found that giving teens meaningful, concrete ways to live their faith in the world, by participating in faith-based service projects or ministry work, was an incredibly important part of helping kids own their faith (Smith, 2014). How much better to be able to make this an essential part of your family life.

Family Mission Statement

One other way to develop your family's sense of Christian mission is to develop a family mission statement. We discuss this a great deal in our book *Parenting with Grace*.

Too often, families think of "service" and "mission" as something that happens outside the home. We discount the million or so ways we can grow in holiness by being kind or generous or responsible or loving or joyful in the home! St. Thérèse of Lisieux advanced the "little way" of holiness. Every task, even the most mundane tasks of washing dishes, taking turns, stating requests kindly, being patient, letting someone else have his way, and looking for ways to make each other's days a little easier or more pleasant can be a path to sainthood if we dedicate these tasks to God and use them as an instrument of our perfection in grace!

That can seem like hard work, and it certainly is the work of a lifetime, but one way to make the path toward this goal clearer and simpler is by developing a family mission statement. There are two parts to this.

Family Mission Statement, Part 1

To begin, sit down with your kids and consider both the qualities or virtues that come more naturally to your family or the qualities or virtues you would need to respond more effectively to the challenges you face as a family. For instance, perhaps you are a very joyful family that likes to tell jokes and laugh a lot together. And you are also a family that has a hard time staying on top of your various household tasks. Combining these strengths and challenges, you might say that your mission was to "be a family that strives to serve God by being joyful and good stewards of all that we have been given." Or, let's say that your family is very hard-working, but you also struggle with bickering. Combining these strengths and challenges, your mission statement might say that your family is committed to "serving God through diligence and by being peacemakers."

In creating your mission statement, celebrate the virtues that come more naturally to you as well as the primary virtues you aspire to — that is, the qualities that would help you be more of the family you'd like to be as well as the qualities that make you proud of the family you are. Although you might wish to master all the virtues (as we all are called to do), your mission statement should represent the two to four virtues that you would most like your family to be identified with.

Once you've identified your short list of virtues, write them as a statement along the lines of the examples we gave above. If you have younger children, it can be fun to have them create a family crest with symbols and pictures that represent the qualities your family has chosen as the heart of your mission. Post this statement or crest in a place in your home where it can be easily seen.

Next, each family member, beginning with the parents, should identify one or two specific things to work on to demonstrate more of that quality in your lives. For instance, if generosity is one of the qualities of your mission, Dad might say that he is going to make a point of initiating a family game time after work even on the days when he's tired. Older Brother might resolve to set the table without being asked, and Little Sister might say that she is going to give others first choice of what to do instead of getting upset when she doesn't get her way. Write these resolutions down.

Finally, several times a week, if not daily, briefly discuss at dinner how everyone is doing in living up to these goals. Talk a bit about what makes it hard to stick to your plan and how you can help each other stay on course. When you've mastered those resolutions, pick new ones and continue the conversation. This way, your family will be regularly committed to little ways you can help, support, and encourage each other to grow in virtue. This is one way that your family can practice the solidarity Catholic families are called to in *The Gospel of Life*, by helping each other use the little tasks and interactions in the daily life of your family as an opportunity to become the people God is calling you to be.

Family Mission Statement, Part 2

The second way you can develop your family mission statement is through regular *virtue practice*. Although your statement will be made up of the virtues that are most important to your family identity, you will probably want to focus on developing other virtues from time to time. For example, if you are being a little short or rude to each other, you might want to focus on developing "respect" over the course of a week or two. Alternatively, if your family has been going through a particularly difficult time, you might want to focus on little things you can do to be more joyful. Choose a virtue for the week. Then, as above, have each person, beginning with the parents, identify a particular resolution that goes with that virtue. Finally, spend a little time each day (or at least several times a week) discussing your efforts to live up to those goals and finding ways you can better support and encourage each other in this pursuit.

If you do this regularly, the entire conversation—on both your mission-statement resolutions and the specific virtue you are practicing in a given week—might take five to ten minutes of your dinnertime. That said, this exercise can be a simple way to help your family dinner discussions revolve around more mean-ingful topics than who needs to go where this evening. Discussing your family mission and the ways you can support each other in living it out will also strengthen your sense of team spirit as you help each other grow in positive ways. Although parents should expect to lead this discussion, be sure to ask your kids what quali-ties they would like to see you practice from week to week. This should grow into an activity that the whole family gives input on.

Fostering Your Children's Sense of Mission

Talk with your children about how they are living your family mission and the virtues you are practicing from week to week when they are at school, at various activities, and with friends. Some readers might think that it is unreasonable to expect chil-dren to try to remember to live out these qualities in every aspect of their lives. Although it may certainly be unrealistic to ask them to live out these qualities perfectly, that is not the point. The goal is to give you the opportunity to disciple your children further by discussing the challenges they face as they try to be intentional Christian young men and women in every part of their lives. When you have these conversations, work hard to avoid lecturing. Do your best to give advice as a last resort. In-stead, focus on listening and asking thoughtful questions that guide your children to finding their own answers. For instance, "What do you think the more respectful thing to do would be?" "If you could have been at your best, how do you think you would have handled that?" "What do you think someone who knew how to be [fill in the virtue] in that situation would have done?"

Obviously, there will be times when it is clear that your chil-dren want or need more direct advice, but the more you work to help them figure things out for themselves, the more they will come to internalize their faith and morals instead of just doing what you tell them to do. This is called developing your children's *internal locus of control*—that is, helping your children take responsibility for thinking through and applying their faith to the challenges of their lives instead of just jumping through your hoops until you're not looking.

The earlier you begin having these discussions, the more your children will be confirmed in their sense of mission by the time they reach high school and college, and the more you can be confident that your children will live their faith in an authentic and meaningful way even as their peers are falling away from the Church.

Your Child's Personal Mission Statement

In addition to having regular conversations about how your children are living out your family mission and the virtues you are practicing in the world, when a child hits the preteen and teen years, it can be helpful to talk him through the steps of developing a personal mission statement.

The basic outline is similar to the steps of developing your family charism and mission statement. Regarding fostering your child's charisms, look at those natural gifts, talents, and abilities that begin to emerge as your child matures. As these become more evident, usually by junior high and certainly by high school, be sure to have conversations with your child about how he can place these gifts in God's service either in whole or in part.

For instance, a preteen or teen who is good at sports can be encouraged to be an example of good sportsmanship and inspiration to his teammates and can be respectful in his dealings with his opponents. A young person who is good at music or reading might be encouraged to become more involved in the parish music ministry or lectoring. A youth who is a good listener might be encouraged to visit the local nursing home. A young person who is creative or gifted at crafts might be encouraged to help out in the parish religious-education program or sell some of his work and donate the proceeds to a charity. Likewise, a youth who is a hard worker could be encouraged to volunteer some of his skills to help a neighbor or the parish or another worthy institution. Encouraging your child to give his gifts back to God allows God to bless those gifts and help your child learn how to find himself in being a blessing to others.

When it comes to helping your preteen or teen develop a personal mission statement, ask your young person what qualities he might like to be most known for by others. It is up to us, as God's children, to be conscious of the message God wants to send to the world through our lives. We do that by being mindful of the qualities and virtues we most wish to be identified with and making both small and big decisions in life with those qualities in mind.

Once you have identified two to four qualities that your child would most like to be known for, be sure to refer back to those qualities during your conversations with your child. For instance, "You've said that you want to be a responsible person. What do you think it would mean to be responsible in that situation?" "You told me that your faith is important to you. What would a person whose faith was important to him decide about this?" "I know you want to be known as a generous person. What do you think the generous thing to do in this situation would be?"

By having regular conversations about the qualities your child has listed as part of his personal mission and making those qualities the starting point for discussions about difficult topics and discipline issues, you have a way of discipling your child into discovering and living out his identity in Christ. This helps to secure attachment through adolescence as your child will come to see you as a person who truly knows what is important to him and always advises him in a manner that is consistent with becoming the person he wants to be. You might be surprised at the willingness of an adolescent to make hard moral choices for himself when he isn't told to do it but instead is led to it by your helping him see how certain choices and relationships allow him to live up to his ideals while others do not. For more discussion on the idea of developing personal mission statements with teens, see *Parenting with Grace*.

Conclusion

In this chapter, we have focused on the importance of living your faith in every part of your life and helping your children learn to do the same. When our experience or the practice of our faith is limited to the four walls of a church building, our children will often lose interest by the time they hit adolescence, if not before. As you discovered earlier, teens in the Relationship-Based Faith Stage are most concerned with how their faith impacts their lives and relationships in the "real world." A faith that's tied to the church building, no matter how great the music is or how dynamic the parish experience may be, is, generally speaking, simply not compelling enough to remain relevant through adolescence, when the child is primarily concerned with developing an identity, seeking causes to serve, and learning how relationships work.

Helping your children develop a charism and mission statement, first by living this out as a family and then by walking your children through the steps of doing this for themselves, enables them to understand, on an experiential level, that their faith can have a powerful, positive impact on every aspect of their lives. It will give them a broad and deep faith that can help them rise to all the challenges they face as they become young men and women. It will give them a faith that they can truly call their own in real, significant, and meaningful ways.

9

Calling All Dads
(and the Women Who Love Them):
Your Mission, Should You Choose to Accept It ...

If there is one point of agreement in virtually all the research on passing the faith on to our children, it is this: fathers are critical. Consider some of the following facts from a major study on faith transition (Craven, 2011).

- If both father and mother attend church regularly, 33 percent of their children will end up as regular church-goers, and 41 percent will end up attending irregularly. Only a quarter of their children will end up not practicing at all.

- If the father is irregular and mother regular, only 3 percent of their children will subsequently become regulars themselves, and a further 59 percent will become irregulars. Thirty-eight percent will be lost.

- If the father is nonpracticing and the mother regular, only 2 percent of their children will become regular worshippers, and 37 percent will attend irregularly. Over 60 percent of their children will be lost completely to the Church!

What happens if the father is regular but the mother irregular or nonpracticing? Amazingly, the percentage of children becoming regular goes up from 33 percent to 38 percent with the irregular mother and up to *44 percent with the nonpracticing mother*.

This can be confusing at first. Why, for instance, do rates of faith retention increase when just fathers attend church compared with when mothers and fathers go together? The most likely answer based on the available data is that a certain percentage of men attending church are dragged there by their wives. The fact that religious retention rates for children are so much higher when the man attends church despite his nonpracticing wife suggests that it is not just whether the father goes to church but his *level of commitment* that determines the ownership his children eventually claim over their faith. Although the study did not examine this, we presume that if the authors looked at how parents' commitment levels impacted faith development, churchgoing mothers and fathers who also had high personal religious commitment would be the subgroup with the highest percentage of children who retained their faith into adulthood.

Building on this, another major study looked at why some people, at great risk to their own lives, were willing to rescue Jews during the Nazi persecution in World War II (Oliner and Oliner, 1988). The study found that the single most significant factor in determining whether a person would be a rescuer, a bystander (who saw the persecution but did nothing), or a collaborator (participant in the persecution) was both the degree of the father's involvement in the passing on of values and the way he did it. Children raised in households where the mother was primarily responsible for character formation tended to be bystanders. Children raised in homes where the fathers were primarily responsible for character formation but used harsh discipline tended to participate in the persecution because, the authors explain, the father's hard discipline tended to emphasize blind obedience, which taught children to follow authority unquestioningly as adults. It was only children who were raised in households where the father was primarily responsible for character formation and he used gentle, loving, relationship-based approaches to discipline (i.e., explaining, teaching, modeling, loving guidance) who grew up to have the courage actively to resist the Nazis. Again, the authors of the study explain that fathers who used gentle discipline methods taught their children moral reasoning instead of blind obedience, and this gave them the ability, as adults, to recognize and resist the influence of unjust authority.

Finally, the largest and most comprehensive study to date, involving 3,500 individuals over forty years, confirmed that the two most important factors in the transmission of faith from parents to children are *parental warmth* (which we discussed in an earlier chapter), and the *father's level of religious commitment* (Bengtson, 2013).

Why Do Dads Matter So Much?

There are no definitive answers as to why fathers are so important for faith transition. Theoretically, however, fathers represent the outside world to the child. Because of this, fathers, more than mothers, are seen by their children as the parent who is responsible for teaching them what it takes to function successfully in the world at large.

On the face of it, this can seem like a sexist, culturally based argument that assumes a stay-at-home mother, but the truth goes much deeper. For the first few years of life, children believe — to varying degrees as they move through toddlerhood — that they and their mother are the same person. They literally think of their mother as a part of themselves. This is not so odd. Remember, a baby starts life inside the mother and very much a part of the mother. Seen from this perspective, the father is the first "other" the child encounters and on a very deep psychological level, the father is responsible—from the earliest days of the child's life—for creating the internal map the child follows for relating to everything outside himself and his home. If faith is not part of the map that the father draws for relating to the outside world, the child simply doesn't grow up to see it as an essential part of life outside himself and his home.

This theory is further supported by the fact that, historically, children who fell away from the faith have tended to return to the faith once they had their own children and home took center stage once again. We say "historically" because in recent years this tendency to return to church after the birth of children is dropping off, presumably since—with the breakup of so many families and the subsequent decrease in cohesive family religious involvement—church is a much less important factor in many mothers' lives as well.

Regardless of the actual reasons, if parents want their children to own their faith, the researchers almost universally agree that fathers must take the lead in everything we are discussing in this book. The more fathers are involved in passing on the faith in both warm and engaging ways, the more important and relevant their children will come to see the faith in their own lives.

What's Mom's Role?

None of this is to say that mothers play no role in their children's faith development. Mothers are essential in helping to form and teach their children the faith. They simply play a much less significant role in enabling their children to carry those lessons into adulthood. Metaphorically speaking, mothers pack their children's faith lunchbox with lots of good, healthful foods, but fathers have everything to do with whether the children remember to take the lunch to school. Even so, if the mom in our metaphor didn't do her bit, her children wouldn't have at least the potential to be spiritually fed when they left the house. Even in situations where fathers are not involved in the faith, moms' efforts to pass the faith on to their children are not for nothing.

What to Do about Dad?

So, if a father isn't involved in his family's faith or in his children's faith formation, what is a Christian mom to do? She must see it as the marital issue it is.

Remember, regardless of actual religious commitment, when moms and dads at least attended church together (and presumably other faith-related activities), the likelihood of their children's faith retention increased from 2 percent (when Dad doesn't go at all) to 33 percent. That's a significant jump to get from just having your husband walk in the door with you. But there is an even bigger point to keep in mind.

It's *really* about respect. It is true that you can't force someone to be a believer and you shouldn't even try. That said, the problem of faith differences in the household are about more basic differences than faith. It is really about respect. When you respect someone, you don't just try to be nice to him, use good manners, and avoid calling him names. You also try to see the truth, goodness, and beauty in all the things the other finds true, good, and beautiful.

You might not love widgets as much as your friend does, but if you love and respect your friend, you don't treat your friend like an idiot for enjoying collecting widgets. You might even try to learn about widgets a bit so that you can understand what your friend is talking about when he shares his love of widgets. Maybe you'd even be willing to go to the widget collector's show when it came to town, at least to keep your friend company. The closer you are to someone, the more you work to respect his interests even when you don't exactly share them.

The same is true when it comes to faith. In her book *When Only One Converts*, Lynn Nordhagen tells the stories of many couples who are in very different places in their faith journeys. These stories reveal that marital harmony is not necessarily dependent on how much the couple sees eye to eye on faith matters. Rather, when a couple does not share their faith, the thing that determines how much conflict this generates appears to be how much the nonpracticing or nonbelieving spouse is willing to support his spouse's faith involvement actively by discussing faith matters, patiently waiting (if not actively participating) during mealtime and other family prayers, and even going to church with his partner.

In our experience, partners who are either hostile toward their mate's faith or passively-aggressively resistant to it demonstrate similar behavior in many other areas of their marriage in which they do not feel as passionately about something that their spouse does. It is extremely rare for a spouse to be disrespectful about his mate's religious involvement without being equally dismissive about his spouse's family commitments or hobbies or interests or the kinds of entertainment his spouse likes that he does not share. This is why we regularly counsel our listeners and clients to reinterpret arguments about religious differences as respect problems.

You cannot force your mate to become a believer, but you can require your mate to respect your faith and your desire to pass your faith on to your children. Practically speaking, that means you have the right to ask your nonbelieving spouse—as a matter of the basic respect one spouse owes to another—at least to accompany you to church and sit respectfully while you say mealtime prayers with your children and even be willing to join you for brief family prayer times.

And for those women who have a believing husband who simply has never been taught to lead prayer or take part in faith discussions, you have a right to expect him to learn, just as, in the course of your marriage, you and your spouse have likely had to learn to do a lot of things: make a budget, cook, do simple home repairs, et cetera.

The bottom line is that dads matter tremendously when it comes to helping children own their faith. It is our deepest hope that men reading this chapter will take our recommendations to heart and begin learning how to take the lead in promoting family prayer and family faith development. It is likewise our deepest hope that wives will stop making excuses for spiritually lazy or disrespectful husbands and will challenge them to be the men of God they are called to be, men who will able to stand confidently before God, knowing that they did everything in their power to give their children the most important relationship of all: a relationship with their heavenly Father.

10

For Families with Particular Struggles:
Faith Development in Divorced
and Single-Parent Households

In the last chapter, we discussed the importance of a father's involvement in the transmission of faith to children. Of course, many children grow up in homes where both parents are not or cannot be involved in their day-to-day lives. What can divorced or single parents do to increase the likelihood that their children will own their faith?

Although the ideal path to leading children to the faith is one in which a warm, highly committed and engaged mother and father work together to bring their children to God, it is not the only path. In the book *Young Catholic America: Emerging Adults In, Out of, and Gone from the Church*, sociologist Christian Smith observes seven pathways by which children may grow up to be religious themselves (2014). There are, of course, other ways children grow up to be faithful, but they are not consistently reliable paths. Smith's research identifies the seven basic paths that lead to a greater likelihood that children will become faithful adults.

The first two pathways involve the kinds of factors we've discussed at length in this book: two highly religiously committed parents who have warm relationships with their children and are actively engaged in their children's faith formation.

A third pathway involves a teen who has relationships with many faithful adults (other than parents) and regularly reads Scripture.

The fourth and fifth pathways involve teens of varying degrees of personal faith who have relationships with many faithful adults, attends some form of regular religious education (either Sunday school or other), and have had some sort of personal religious experience.

A sixth pathway involves a teen who has little religious exposure or training at home or little outside exposure to religion or religious support but has had several personal meaningful religious experiences (for instance, because of attending a youth group or youth conference on a whim and then attending faithfully after experiencing an initial spiritual encounter).

The final pathway involves a teen who has little personal faith but has had regular exposure to Scripture, followed at some point by a series of personally meaningful religious experiences.

Based on this, there are a few recommendations we can make to divorced and single parents to help increase the likelihood that your children will remain faithful into adulthood.

Model a real-life faith. You can't give what you don't have. Work hard to be not only pious but serious about applying your faith to your life and relationships. You cannot allow your faith simply to be the thing you escape into as a refuge from your stressful life. It is critical that you let your faith inspire you to become that warm, loving, virtuous parent who is an example to your children of what it means to live an authentic life as a Christian person. You don't have to be perfect or pretend to be, but you have to allow yourself to become radically open to God's grace in a way that allows you to be as authentic and loving as possible. This is the kind of faith that allows you to face challenges in an admirable way and create a discipleship relationship with your child. The previous chapters on family mission and family prayer will be of particular importance in this regard.

Foster regular spiritual rituals. Earlier in the book, we discussed the importance of rituals and routines. This will be doubly important for you, especially when it comes to regular family prayer times and reading Scripture together as a family (recall our discussion of Bible stories in the section on stages of faith). Only about 15 percent of separated or divorced Catholics pray with their children (Gray and Gaunt, 2015). It will be tremendously important for you to work against this trend in your home. Regular time for family prayer, family worship, and family Scripture reading is critical for the divorced or single parent who wishes to raise faithful kids.

Create community. Create a community of faithful adults to support you. Let your children see and learn personally from other adults who live the faith. The more they see how the faith makes a real, practical, powerful difference in the life, choices, and quality of relationships of the other adults and families in your life, the more your children will relate to your faith not as a curious hobby but as the path to a full and enriching life.

Facilitate spiritual experiences. Do what you can to make faith a real, meaningful, and personal part of your daily relationship with your child. Make sure your prayer life with your child incorporates the joys, concerns, and needs that are part of their everyday life. Talk openly about answered prayers. Pray over your child.

Bring your child to conferences and events where you and your child can have meaningful and personal encounters with the Holy Spirit and feel the presence of God in your lives. Later, give your teen lots of opportunities to have these kinds of experiences with his peers at various youth conferences and other events.

Create opportunities to serve. In our discussion of relationship-based faith (in the chapter on stages of faith), we examined the importance of religious causes to help pass on the faith. Teens want to make a difference in the world. For the young adult, especially, nothing is relevant if it doesn't positively impact the lives and relationships of others. A faith that makes a difference in the lives of the people around a teen is a faith worth clinging to. Get involved with your child in faith-based service projects, and give your teens lots of opportunities to get involved in such projects on his own when he gets older.

Regular religious education. In addition to living out the faith at home, which is absolutely critical, do whatever you can to make sure that your child is involved in parish-based religious education either in a Catholic school or at least in "Sunday school." This provides additional support for the work that you are doing at home and increases the likelihood that your child will experience other adults and peers for whom the faith is important.

Between Two Worlds: A Word for Divorced Parents

In addition to the above, divorced parents need to be aware of another dynamic. In her book, *Between Two Worlds: The Inner Lives of Children of Divorce* and her follow up video, *Between Two Worlds: The Spiritual Lives of Children of Divorce* (2013), Elizabeth Marquardt notes that even in the best circumstances—where a child of divorce has a good relationship with both the mother and the father—there can be significant spiritual fallout. This is because divorce forces children to live between two worlds that never come together except in their own heads. When they are with Mom, they tend not to talk about life with Dad, their friends, activities, rules, and so forth, for fear of upsetting Mom. When they are with Dad, they tend not to talk about life with Mom. This often causes children of divorce never to feel "at home."

This applies to church too. Assuming both Mom and Dad go to church, people in Dad's church—including pastors—are reluctant to talk about the child's life with Mom, for fear of offending Dad. And at Mom's church, people—including pastors—are reluctant to talk about life with Dad for fear of offending Mom. And, of course, if either Mom or Dad doesn't go to church, it looks to the child as if church is a hobby that one parent enjoys rather than a way of life.

The result is that the child never gets to feel as if his whole life ever really comes together in any place except inside his head. Even spirituality, which is supposed to be a source of finding meaning, purpose, and direction in life (Pargament, 2011), becomes a source of division. This dynamic can lead to a life of spiritual ambivalence in which the child never really trusts anyone besides himself to help him make sense out of life (Pargament, 2011).

What can you do? Keep the lines of communication as open as possible between you, your ex, and your child. Don't grill your child about time with your ex, but make sure that you allow your child to feel comfortable about sharing the things that go on when he is visiting your ex. When possible, work with your ex to give your child a consistent spiritual home. It might not be advisable to go church together, but perhaps you could go to different Masses at the same parish. Or, make one parish the child's home parish where your child regularly worships and goes to school or Sunday school. Your ex can take the child there but go to another parish on your "off" weekends. Let the parish be the one place where the two worlds your child straddles come together as much as possible. Beyond this, keep rules and rituals (especially spiritual rituals) as consistent as possible between the two households. Encourage your child to pray about the things that go on when he is visiting your ex, to give thanks for the good things, and to ask for grace to deal with concerns.

In short, divorced parents can help their children see their faith and spiritual lives as a resource for helping them gracefully negotiate the two worlds they live in, increasing the likelihood that their children will grow up seeing the Church as a genuine help, instead of just one more thing that divides their family and their lives.

It isn't easy to raise faithful kids without a partner, but it absolutely can be done. By modeling and sharing a personal faith, creating rituals that give order and meaning to your life with your child, creating a community that helps to give your child experiences of other adults who take the faith seriously, and doing what you can to facilitate up-close-and-personal encounters with God for your child, your faith can help bring deeper meaning, order, peace, and grace to your life and your child's.

Part 3

Meet the Family:
Connecting Kids to the Community of Faith

Raising faithful kids is a tough job. Fortunately, you don't have to do it alone. Your parish community wants to help you and your children discover God together so that you can live your faith and every other part of your life more abundantly.

In part 3 of *Discovering God Together* we look at how participating in the life of the Church, in the sacraments, and in other ways can facilitate a strong connection between you, your children, and God.

11

I Call You By Name:

Getting More Out of Baptism

The sacraments are an essential part of your child's participation in God's Family, the Church. Obviously, participating in God's Family is not like participating in any earthly club or organization. There is something deeper and more meaningful going on; something that doesn't just begin and end with us. Rather, our participation in the life of the Church begins with an invitation from God to become his children. We say yes to that invitation through our participation in the sacraments — in particular, the Sacraments of Initiation: Baptism, the Eucharist, and Confirmation.

This chapter will look briefly at Baptism, how you can explain it to your children, and how you can celebrate the significance of this great sacrament in your life and the lives of your children. The next two chapters will take a similar approach to the remaining Sacraments of Initiation. For additional information on preparing for Baptism and getting more out of the experience of the sacrament, see our book *Then Comes Baby: The Catholic Guide to Surviving and Thriving in the First Three Years of Parenting.*

Discovering God Together

What Baptism Does

Baptism represents our first yes to God's invitation to become his sons and daughters. Many of us were baptized as infants, and our parents, by saying yes to God for us, promised to teach us what it means to live as his children. Baptism does three things: it frees us from sin, enables us to be reborn as sons and daughters of God, and makes us part of God's Family, which also commits us to the family business — as it were — which is to build the Kingdom of God.

With Baptism, your child has been given an incredible gift. Your child is transformed into a son or daughter of God! You will need to spend your life teaching your child how to appreciate this awesome gift so that he always remembers who he is. As a baptized person, your child is destined for an eternal life of happiness with God and the Communion of Saints.

Celebrating Your Spiritual Birthday

As such, Baptism is something to celebrate and continue celebrating throughout your life, just as you celebrate your birthday. In fact, in some ways, it is even more important than celebrating your birthday. The celebration of your physical birthday comes to an end when you pass away, but because Baptism represents your birth into the Family of God, this is one birthday we hope you and your children will celebrate for all eternity! Here are a few ideas to get you started.

Bring out the pictures. Do you have pictures of your Baptism? Displaying in your home even small pictures of your Baptism and of your children's baptisms can be a great reminder of that most important day. You'd be surprised how many spontaneous faith discussions are prompted when kids see these pictures.

Getting More Out of Baptism

Think about getting copies of your baptismal certificates from the parishes where you, your spouse, and your children were baptized and having them framed.

Use holy-water fonts in your home. When we go into church, we dip our fingers into the holy-water font and make the Sign of the Cross as a reminder of our baptism. You can get small, inexpensive holy-water fonts to place in your room and your children's rooms and even near the front door of your home. Getting into the habit of blessing yourself with holy water when you leave your room or your home in the morning will remind your family that your Baptism makes you a child of God and that God is asking you to bring honor to his family name as you go about your school and work days.

Celebrate your patron saints' feast days. Although it isn't necessary, the Church strongly encourages the faithful to take the name of a saint who will be their special patron and will pray for them throughout their lives before God. Historically, a patron was someone who spoke for you to the king, who supported your work in some way, and who served to make your way in life smoother. A patron saint will pray for you before the King of heaven and earth, support and inspire you in your work of building the Kingdom of God, and help make your faith journey smoother both through his example and his prayers. Even if you weren't named for a saint — or don't know which saint you were named for — you can still choose a patron saint; someone whose example inspires you and whose intercession you would value. To choose a patron saint, simply ask that saint to be your patron and regularly talk to him in your prayer time.

Once you have chosen a special saint to be your patron, be sure to celebrate your relationship with that saint. If possible, go to Mass on your saint's feast day. Perhaps you can have a special meal on that day. For younger children, it can be fun to do a craft project that reflects some aspect of the patron saint's life and ministry. You might even obtain a relic—for instance, a small piece of an object that was touched by your patron saint—to serve as a physical reminder of that saint's presence in your life. All of these ideas, and others like them, can be wonderful ways to remind yourself and your children to follow the example of your older brothers and sisters in the Lord.

Have a Baptism-day party. Having a Baptism-day party can be a wonderful way to celebrate your Baptism. If possible, go to Mass as a family on that day. Have a special meal with a special dessert to celebrate the sweetness of God's love and grace. It can be meaningful to give a small, spiritually themed gift on this day; something that can help your child in his prayer life or faith development, such as a new rosary or Bible or another faith-based gift that will have some significance for your child. Celebrate this day for the special gift that it is. Incidentally, Baptism-day parties aren't just for kids. Parents should make sure to celebrate their Baptism day too as a sign to their children of the ongoing importance of their baptismal identity.

Do your own thing. As we said at the beginning of this list, there aren't any official rules for celebrating your Baptism day. What are some ways you can think of that would be special for your family to celebrate your Baptism days? Make a list of your ideas.

Conclusion

It might seem strange or overly pious to celebrate your Baptism or patronal feast day, especially if you didn't grow up doing it. Remember that these ideas are not about putting on spiritual airs or pretending to be holier than other families on your block or in your parish. These are all just different ways you can bring a little more joy and grace into your life and say that your faith is something worth celebrating. As far as we're concerned, we can always use another reason to celebrate in our lives. What better reason to celebrate than the gift of becoming a child of God?

Remember that although we all benefit from physical reminders of our faith, younger children in particular benefit from tangible reminders that God and their faith life have a real and positive impact on their daily lives. Celebrating the day on which your child became a child of God is a wonderful way to make a positive impression on your child of the importance of living his Christian identity in every aspect of his life. With a little thought and creativity, you can transform the occasion of your child's Baptism from a once-in-a-lifetime event into an ongoing reminder of what it means to be and live as a child of God.

12

Up Close and Personal:
Getting More from Your Family's
Encounter with Christ in the Eucharist

All the sacraments help us encounter Christ, but the Eucharist is the single most important way we can experience Christ as our Savoir and Redeemer. The *Catechism* tells us that the Eucharist is "the source and summit of the Christian life" (no. 1324). In other words, the Eucharist is where we most personally and meaningfully encounter Christ.

It would not be making too much of this sacrament to say that the entirety of your child's Catholic faith relies on whether he "gets" the personal significance of receiving Jesus Christ, Body, Blood, soul, and divinity. We as Catholic parents have no job more important than helping our children fall in love with Christ in the Eucharist. Most Catholic parents seem to intuit this. In fact, according to a study by CARA/Holy Cross Family Ministries, 66 percent of Catholic parents believe it is "very important" that their children make their First Communion, and 83 percent believe that it is at least "somewhat important" (Gray and Gaunt, 2015).

Growing up in the United States, Catholics often encounter our Evangelical Protestant brothers and sisters in the Lord who ask us, "Have you accepted Jesus Christ into your heart as your personal Lord and Savior?" Every Catholic can and must answer this question emphatically and affirmatively. "Yes! Because I receive our Lord in the Eucharist, I have not only accepted Jesus Christ into my heart as my personal Lord and Savior, but God has made me his very own flesh and blood! He has united his flesh with mine, and his blood courses through my veins. I am his, and he is mine, and we are one because his flesh is real food and his blood is real drink, and I have new life in him!"

Such a statement is not over the top. In fact, it probably isn't extreme enough when you consider the incredible gift that the Eucharist truly is and the significance it has for the life of the Christian person. Jesus himself told us that the Eucharist is absolutely essential for salvation. "[U]nless you eat the flesh of the Son of man and drink his blood, you have no life in you" (John 6:53).

The Fruits of the Sacrament

In this chapter, we will look at the purpose of the Eucharist and ways you and your children can get more out of your family's experience of this sacrament. We'll also offer some tips on getting more out of your experience of bringing small children to Mass.

According to the *Catechism*, the Eucharist bears several fruits in our life and the life of the Church: it strengthens our union with Christ (no. 1391); separates us from sin (no. 1393); unites each person who receives Jesus Christ in the sacrament with every other person—both in this life and the next—who has received him in the Eucharist (no. 1396); and nourishes charity (no. 1397).

Your Family's Encounter with Christ in the Eucharist

How You Can Get More out of Your Experience

We hope the following suggestions, intended as a response to the four fruits the Eucharist bears, will serve as a springboard for your creativity, giving you some basic suggestions that can inspire you and your children to think of more ways you can experience the graces of the Eucharist in the daily life of your domestic church.

Name the miracle. It can be tough to bring small children to Mass. Although it can be counterintuitive to do so, it truly is helpful to sit up front as a family because it enables children to see what's going on. Additionally, parents can make their lives easier by having a special activity bag filled with quiet, faith-based toys (religious picture books, soft Bible-figure dolls) that can be reserved as special "going to church" activities.

That said, whatever else you might do, we invite parents to stop everything they or their children are doing at the time of the Elevation (the point when the priest raises the host and the chalice after saying the words of institution, "This is my body" and "This is my blood") and call their attention to the miracle at the altar. For your smaller children, hold them on your lap or — if you are kneeling — lift them up so they can see the altar. When the priest raises first the host and then the chalice, whisper lovingly in your child's ear, "Look at the miracle! The bread and wine is becoming Jesus. Can you say, "I love you, Jesus'?" Have your child *quietly* say those words. This simple action helps to highlight the importance of the Consecration even for your youngest children and helps them realize that something truly special is going on. We did this with our children from the day they were born. Starting as early as possible — even before your children understand what you are saying — establishes a habit of acknowledging the Presence of the Lord. It sends the message to even your very young children that something special is happening that is deserving of their attention. (For additional tips on getting more out of taking your infants and toddlers to Mass, see our book *Then Comes Baby: The Catholic Guide to Surviving and Thriving in the First Three Years of Parenthood*.)

Older children and adults can model their own sign of reverence at this time, bowing their heads, or praying silently words such as "My Lord and My God" or even striking their breast—a traditional Roman sign of respect. The moment of the Consecration is, literally, a miraculous moment. Cultivate the attentiveness, respect, and honor it deserves by teaching even your youngest children to be aware of the miracle.

Approach with respect. Teach your children to receive the Precious Body and Blood of Jesus with respect, and model that respect in your own reception of the Eucharist. As you go up in line, use that time to pray, either by joining in the song the congregation is singing (as St. Augustine put it, "To sing is to pray twice") or by offering yourself to the Lord and asking him to open your heart to receive him totally and be transformed by his love.

Teach your children how you pray in line as you go up to receive the Lord. Resist the temptation to chat in line or wave at others you know as you go up to Communion. Yes, the Eucharist has a communal dimension, and it is not simply a "me and Jesus" experience, but we are sharing that communion by focusing on the Eucharist together, not by being a distraction to others or distracting ourselves from the important mysteries in which we are participating.

If your children are disrespectful in the Communion line—either by galumphing back to the pew or by making the experience about communing with other kids more than with the Lord, correct them *gently* by reminding them of the importance of the Eucharist. Take a few minutes after Mass to lead your children lovingly and gently in a prayer in which they offer a simple apology to God for taking his gift of grace for granted. This is to be a time not of humiliation or anger but of loving correction and guidance. Make sure to hug them afterward and let them know that you are confident in their ability to do better next time and, if necessary, remind them gently what you expect the next time you are at Mass.

Adore the Lord. One thing that we and many faithful parents we know have found tremendously helpful for deepening our experience of the Eucharist is to bring children to some form of adoration, whether that is formal adoration of the Blessed Sacrament or simply popping into your Church's Eucharistic chapel for five to ten minutes for an impromptu visit with Jesus.

Taking time for adoration of the Eucharist does not detract from the need to receive the Eucharist any more than staring into eyes of your beloved detracts from your desire to kiss and hold your beloved. In fact, we have found that taking even brief times to gaze into the face of our heavenly Beloved increases the seriousness and meaningfulness of our children's experience of receiving the Eucharist. If you do this as a family, take a few minutes ahead of time to talk to your kids about the best way to use this time. They may, for example, read a children's Bible, pray a decade of the Rosary (help them pick one of the mysteries), use something like the PRAISE format we discussed earlier, or just look at Jesus and tell him from their heart how much they love him.

If you also want a more formal experience of Eucharistic adoration, find out when your parish offers this and go together as a family. Children are often deeply moved by the mystery and reverence surrounding adoration. It can be a beautiful and moving experience even for young children. Make sure to discuss it with them afterward and elicit their experience as well as sharing yours.

You might be interested in starting a Children of Hope chapter in your parish. This international program encourages a children's version of Eucharistic adoration that is both reverent and relevant for even the youngest children. In fact, it is meant for kids as young as toddlers. Learn more at www.ChildrenofHope.org.

Build your domestic church. As we observed earlier, the *Catechism* states that the "Eucharist makes Church." Let the Eucharist strengthen the bonds of your domestic church. Each Sunday, go to Mass as a family and make a point of doing activities afterward that build communion between you and your children. Many families go out to breakfast after Mass, and we encourage this, but perhaps you can do even a little more by making each Sunday a full family day that begins with a celebration of the Eucharist—the one time all week when you get to be together all day and celebrate your life as a family. Whether you have a picnic or take a hike, or ride bikes together, or go to a movie or a play, or play board games or take in a sporting event, do it together and let the Eucharist be the beginning and inspiration for greater communion in your domestic church. The more you do this, the more you build an emotional connection between your child's experience of the Eucharist and the sense of anticipation and togetherness that your family experiences together.

In discussing this kind of family time with your kids, make sure they understand that you are not asking them to "get through Mass" so that you can "get to" the fun parts of the day. Rather, it is your sharing the Eucharist that makes you want to take time together as a family as a way of giving thanks to God for all he has given you. Resist becoming involved in any activities that threaten your ability to take this regular time together after Mass as a family. If you must become involved in something that has events on Sundays, make sure it is something you all enjoy and can do together. But again, it is better to treat Sunday Family Day as a sacred ritual of the domestic church that begins with the celebration of the Eucharist and extends into the fellowship and fun you share all day.

Serve one another. Remember that the *Catechism* says that the Eucharist challenges us to be charitable. It's important to teach our children—and remind ourselves—that it isn't enough to receive the Eucharist; we must also *be eucharistic* to one another. That means that families can use the Eucharist as an inspiration to find ways to make each other's days easier and more pleasant.

You can do this more formally by using the virtue-training and mission-building exercises we discussed in an earlier chapter. When asking your kids which qualities they would like to practice as a family, you might set this discussion up by asking, "How can we be eucharistic this week? How can we be Jesus to each other?" Then discuss ways you can make a gift of yourselves to each other just as Jesus makes a gift of himself to us in the Eucharist.

This might sound too pious or sophisticated for young minds to grasp, but we have found that children really respond to these discussions, and the younger, the better. Children naturally want to learn how to please Mom and Dad, how to please God, how to get along with each other, and how to use their gifts and abilities to contribute to family life. The younger the children are, the less likely they are to have had this impulse socialized out of them by a world that prefers selfishness to self-giving. Teaching this language, and the resolutions that go along with it, to your young children will help them learn to resist the temptation to think they are too cool to care about others.

As we discussed in the chapter on mission, it can also be helpful to choose various service projects that your family can do together as a way of giving back to your parish or your community. That said, there is wisdom in the saying that charity begins in the home. We know too many families who are happy to volunteer in the parish or in the community but don't make serving each other in the family a priority. This can lead children to think that faith is a service project, not the source of transformation of hearts and relationships. Any service you do for the community should stand as an expansion of the loving service you already offer one another in your home, not as a replacement for it.

Conclusion

These are just a few ways you can more effectively live out the call to unity, church, community, and charity that the Eucharist extends to your family. We hope that these ideas will inspire you to identify even more ways to experience more fully the transformative power of the Eucharist.

Regardless, the most important takeaway from this chapter is the idea that the Eucharist is not just something you do at Mass and then forget about by the time you leave the church parking lot. The Eucharist is the source and summit of your faith and the power source that informs everything else you do as a family to draw closer to Christ and each other throughout the week. This is the single most important lesson you can convey to your children.

Your Family's Encounter with Christ in the Eucharist

In our own experience as a family, there have been many times when we and our children wrestled with doubts or struggled with this teaching or that, or this or that problem with the Church. Faith and struggle is a natural part of anyone's faith journey. Through it all, the one thing that keeps us and our kids coming back to church, no matter what the struggle du jour might be, is a deep love for Christ in the Eucharist. We are often reminded of the words of the apostles, who, when asked by Jesus if they, too, would leave him, as some of his other disciples had, answered, "Lord, to whom shall we go?" (cf. John 6:66–68).

No matter how exciting the music is at the service of some other denomination, or how dynamic the preaching might be in that non-Catholic church down the street, or how awesome the youth group might be at the little Evangelical church around the corner, or how frustrated we feel about some current struggles we're facing in our relationship with God, at the end of the day, it's the Eucharist that keeps us coming back to the one, holy, catholic, and apostolic Church, because it is the one thing that allows us to be united in the most intimate way possible to the God who loves and sustains us. And, ultimately, that is the only thing that truly matters.

13

Let the Fire Fall:
Confirmed in Your Christian Mission

Confirmation completes in us the work begun in Baptism, deepening our connection to the Family of God, increasing our experience of what it means to live in the Holy Spirit, and confirming us in our membership in the common priesthood of the faithful, whose "job" it is to consecrate the world to Christ in everything we say and do.

No matter when we receive this powerful sacrament, clearly it conveys an important task in the life of the Christian. The following represent some ways you can begin to celebrate the graces of this sacrament more fully in the life of your family. This list is far from complete, but we hope it will serve as a springboard for ongoing discussions in your family about how you can bear witness to the joy of the gospel in your lives.

Family and personal prayer. In earlier chapters, we focused on how to cultivate a vibrant familial and personal prayer life. Nothing can empower your family to experience the fullness of the graces conferred in all the sacraments, especially Confirmation, like a deep and meaningful prayer life. It is the Holy Spirit's role to fill us with the love of the Father and the Son, but we cannot experience the power of this love if we either fail to pray regularly or approach prayer as a chore to be checked off a list.

When you pray, ask God to set your hearts ablaze with the fire of his love so that your home will be warmed by that fire and that all the world will be drawn to God through the light that burns in your hearts and in your home. You may pray this intention in your own words, or you may use the traditional prayer of the Holy Spirit.

> *Come, Holy Spirit, fill the hearts of your faithful and kindle in us the fire of your love. Send forth your Spirit, and we shall be created. And you shall renew the face of the earth. O God, who by the light of the Holy Spirit, did instruct the hearts of the faithful, grant that by the same Holy Spirit we may be truly wise and ever enjoy His consolations. Through Christ our Lord. Amen.*

Every day, make sure you place your hands on your children's heads as a sign of blessing and pray that the Holy Spirit would fill their hearts and minds and set their lives ablaze with the fire of God's love. Then make the Sign of the Cross on their foreheads to remind them of their identity as sons and daughters of God.

Confirm your mission. Regardless of when your children receive Confirmation, they will be better prepared to participate in the grace of the sacrament if you consistently work to live out the recommendations we made previously in our chapter on creating a familial and personal sense of mission. Remember, Confirmation empowers your family to proclaim the love of God with your lives. The way you live as a family and the way you encounter the world should make you stand out — in a good way — not because you are showing off or trying to pretend to be something that you are not, but because you are striving to live a deeper love in your home and in the world.

Remember, too, to expect your children to fulfill their mission to be witnesses. Read them stories of the courageous child saints who lived, and in many cases, willingly died for the sake of the gospel. Remind your children — not in a lecturing way, but in the course of your regular conversations about living your mission as a family and doing the virtue-practice exercise we described in an earlier chapter — that God expects them to "raise the bar" when they are at school or playing with their friends. Children are capable of great spiritual heroism if they are encouraged to exhibit it. That's just one of the reasons Jesus told us that we must become like little children if we are to enter the Kingdom of heaven (see Matt. 18:3). As you talk and pray with your children about their daily lives, make sure to ask them how God would want them to respond to the blessings and challenges they encounter, and gently challenge them to be witnesses to Christian virtue in their dealings with their friends and classmates.

The Church specifically lists twelve fruits of the Holy Spirit — that is, twelve virtues that are evident in people whose faith is authentic and vibrant. These are charity, joy, peace, patience, kindness, goodness, generosity, gentleness, faithfulness, modesty, self-control, and chastity. In your efforts to reflect on your family mission, be sure to encourage your children in developing their own sense of personal mission; and in your family's use of the virtue-practice exercise, consider periodically how each of you is trying to bear witness to these fruits in your life as a family and in your dealings with the outside world. You might even make part of your dinner conversations a reflection on one of these qualities simply by observing, for example, "God really gave me a chance to practice kindness today" and then telling your story.

You can follow up by asking what chances God has given the rest of your family to live out the fruits of the Spirit in their lives.

Take your mission on the road. If your kids are old enough, make volunteer work as a family one of your work rituals. For suggestions on how your family can live its commitment to do good together, check out the website www.BigHeartedFamilies.org. As your children get older and begin developing their interests and hobbies, make sure that you actively encourage them (and even require them) to do regular volunteer and service work. Help them realize that they can make a difference in God's Kingdom at every age!

Engage in spiritual reading as a family. Living the life in the Spirit to which you are called through the sacrament of Confirmation requires ongoing formation. There are some wonderful books that can help you on your journey. Alan Schreck's books *Your Life in the Spirit: What Every Catholic Needs to Know and Experience* and *The Gift: Discovering the Holy Spirit in Catholic Tradition* are terrific resources for preparing for and getting more out of Confirmation. We also highly recommend *Sober Intoxication of the Spirit* (parts 1 and 2) by Fr. Raniero Cantalamessa, former preacher to the papal household of St. John Paul II; *Fruits and Gifts of the Spirit* by Thomas Keating; and *More of the Holy Spirit: How to Keep the Fire Burning in Our Hearts* by Sr. Ann Shields. These are wonderful books for the adults and young adults in your family, but they can also be the source of many dinnertime conversations and prayerful reflections with your kids.

As we said at the outset, this list is not meant to be exhaustive. Rather, we hope it will inspire your creativity and encourage you to lead your children and challenge yourself to go deeper in your faith journey. The Holy Spirit has great plans for you and your family. Let the fire of the Spirit's love warm the heart of your home and enable your family to be a light to the world that brings everyone who meets you a little closer to Christ.

14

Gathering the Lost Lambs:
Experiencing Confession as a Loving Place

Besides the Sacraments of Initiation, one sacrament that is an essential part of fully living out the Christian call to deeper conversion and wholeness is the sacrament of Confession.

Strictly speaking, the law of the Church requires Catholics to go to Confession once a year and then only if we have committed a mortal sin. Venial sins are absolved during the penitential rite of the Mass and do not require us to go to Confession to be healed.

Even so, anyone who is serious about becoming everything God wants him to be does well to make Confession a regular part of his spiritual life. Traditionally, there are two ways to think about sin. In the West, Catholics tend to think of sin in terms of wrongdoing, the breaking of laws, and the imposing of "just punishments." In the Eastern Rites of the Church, Catholics tend to think of sin more in terms of a sickness, and the sacraments — especially Confession — as the treatment for the spiritual diseases that hinder the life of Christ in us.

Cultivating a Healthy Sense of Sin

Although both understandings of sin have value and get at different aspect of the problem of sin, we find that children tend to have a much healthier understanding of sin and a willing attitude toward Confession when parents emphasize the metaphor of sin as a spiritual illness of which we need to be healed.

Saying that sin is a sickness doesn't let us off the hook, of course. When we are sick, we recognize that there are things we must do to get healthy again. We must take our medicine. We must do our exercises. We must rest. But ultimately, we must go to the doctor, who will prescribe a course of treatment. That is what regular Confession is for. Seen in this light, rather than having Confession feel like a sentencing before a judge for our crimes, our experience can be more like that of the person who seeks regular spiritual checkups, during which the Divine Physician (i.e., God) can, through the ministry of the priest, not only cure our illnesses but also make recommendations to help us become even healthier and stronger in the life of grace. Saying that our venial sins are forgiven every time we go to Mass is not the same as saying that we cannot benefit from the additional healing grace and counsel we can receive from regular Confession. The more help we can get to become healthy, strong, vibrant sons and daughters of God, the better!

Here are a few recommendations to help you celebrate the graces of the sacrament of Confession in your domestic church. By no means should this list be considered exhaustive. We simply hope that the following can be the basis of the ongoing discussion in your family on ways you can enter more fully into the mystery and joy of God's everlasting mercy and love.

Go to Confession as a family. In days gone by, in addition to weekly Mass attendance, Catholic families often went to church together once a month so that everyone who was eligible could receive God's forgiveness and love in Confession. Creating a monthly Confession ritual as a family helps to link your family to the life of the Church and normalizes the experience. The more you do something, the more natural it becomes. Likewise, the less you do something, the more ominous and mysterious it feels. Monthly Confession helps us and our children cultivate a habit of getting regular spiritual checkups without allowing us to fall into the problem of scrupulosity (a spiritual disorder that comes from an overactive sense of guilt). When we can go to Confession monthly as a family, Confession loses much of its more negative connotations and becomes a regular and normal tool in our spiritual toolkit. Just as seeking forgiveness from our parents and siblings is a normal and frequent part of family life, seeking forgiveness for the offenses we commit against our brothers and sisters in the Lord is a normal and regular part of the family life of God.

Use positive approaches to discipline at home. Much of our emotional understanding of sin and its cure (Confession) comes from our experience of discipline in our homes. When we broke a rule, did our parents yell, impose harsh punishments, and leave us guessing how we could handle the situation better next time? Or did our parents gently correct our misdeeds, take time to understand the intention behind our foolish behavior, and then teach us more godly and efficient ways to meet those intentions in the future? In our experience, children raised in households who exhibited this latter preference for loving-guidance-oriented discipline approaches are much more willing to admit wrongdoing and seek forgiveness and reconciliation in appropriate and healthy ways than are children who are raised in households with a more punitive approach to discipline. Harsher discipline approaches tend to make children more secretive, less willing to

Discovering God Together

admit wrongdoing, and less likely to seek guidance on how to do better next time. All these attitudes make approaching Confession with an open and willing heart that much more difficult. For specific tips on healthy approaches to positive discipline, see our book *Parenting with Grace*.

Help your kids have a vision of their "best self." In our chapter on guiding your children in developing their own mission statement, we encouraged you to help your children develop a sense of what their "best self" looks like. That is, what are the virtues they would most like to be identified with, and what choices must they make in their daily lives and relationships to increase the likelihood that they will actually come to resemble those virtues and traits they hold dear?

Having this clear, positive sense of who we would like to be, who God is calling us to be, can give us a sense of what we need Confession to help us accomplish. If we know that we want to be thought of as "responsible, respectful, joyful, and generous," we can be more sensitive to opportunities to practice these virtues and more aware of times we struggle to live these qualities out. By helping your child develop a healthy sense of his ideal self, you can simultaneously help him develop a healthy sense of sin. That is, you can help him see sin as less of an occasion of condemnation and more of a testament to our need for God's mercy and assistance in becoming everything we were created to be in this life and ultimately in the next life: "perfect, as our heavenly Father is perfect" (Matt. 5:48).

Develop a positive approach to an examination of conscience. If you have helped your child develop the kind of personal mission statement we discussed earlier in the book and referenced above, you can use it to teach your child a positive approach to

148

the ancient Catholic practice of doing a daily examination of conscience. In an examination of conscience, you take a few moments each day to reflect both on ways that you gave in to temptations to be less than your best self and on ways you might do better tomorrow with God's grace. Unless your child is struggling with a particular sinful habit, we find children tend to do best with daily examinations of conscience that focus on times when they needed to be, for instance, *more* loving, *more* responsible, and *more* generous, et cetera, rather than on times when they *failed to be loving* or *failed to be responsible* or *failed to be generous*, et cetera. Both are correct, but psychologically speaking, the latter can feel less intimidating to children and allow them to approach their sins with a sense of hope and grace rather than a spirit of condemnation and futility.

Forgive willingly. Forgiving willingly is one of the Spiritual Works of Mercy that Christians are called to practice in their everyday lives. Do your best to practice willing forgiveness in your family life. Model forgiveness toward your children, correcting them gently and lovingly without shaming them or humiliating them for their mistakes and wrongdoing. Encourage your children to be similarly generous to each other in seeking forgiveness from and extending forgiveness to one another. Make seeking and extending forgiveness not only as normal a part of family life as possible but as positive and joyful an experience as possible. After you've corrected your children for wrongdoing, be sure to collect your children's hearts by spending a few moments cuddling with them and telling them how proud you are of their willingness to learn better ways to behave and how confident you are in their ability to do better in the future. The efforts you extend toward making the process of correction as positive and affirming as it reasonably can be will go a long way toward helping your children to be willing to seek God's forgiveness regularly.

Again, as in each of our chapters on ways to get more out of the sacraments, the examples we offer here are just to get your own conversations started. Still, even if you begin only with the suggestions we recommend here, you will be helping your children come to experience Confession as an opportunity to celebrate God's mercy and receive the grace they need to become the people he created them to be.

15

The Friends and Family Plan:
Participating in the Life of the Parish and Community

Your parish is your Catholic home away from home and, as such, can be a great support in your efforts to discover God together as a family and raise faithful children. The key word here, however, is *support*. In our experience, too many Catholic families assume that parish life alone will be sufficient for forming their children in the faith. We regularly get calls from heartbroken parents who say that their children were regular Mass attendees and altar servers through high school but then abandoned the faith in college. When we compare the stories of these families with Catholic families whose children remain spiritually engaged in college and even exercise leadership roles in faith groups in their college and young-adult years, the *difference that makes the difference* is almost always the degree to which the faith impacted the relationship quality and daily life of the domestic church.

In some cases, of course, parish life can actually be a threat to faith development. Usually this occurs with well-meaning parents who have a strong sense of the importance of their faith but an overinflated sense of the importance of being involved in parish life. When this happens, the quality of the relationships in the domestic church suffers because volunteering at the parish becomes just one more set of activities, like sports, dance, music, and other classes, that compete for first place with family life.

With those qualifiers in mind, connecting with our parish in healthy and nourishing ways is an essential part of our development as Catholic persons. We are a Church that believes in the importance of communion. Of course, that's true about "communion" as in the Eucharist, but here we mean it in the sense of community. Catholicism is not a "me and Jesus" sort of faith. It isn't even a "me, my family, and Jesus" sort of faith. It is, ultimately a "me and Jesus and the whole Family of God working together, growing together, loving one another and supporting each other as we strive to build the Kingdom in this life and celebrate together in the Communion of Saints in the next" kind of faith. Healthy parish involvement plays an essential role in celebrating the communal dimension of our Catholic faith.

With that in mind, here are some ways you can build a relationship with your parish that can foster the good work you are doing in your home.

Go to Mass together. We've covered this elsewhere in the book, but it bears repeating. With conflicting schedules and the challenge of wrangling small children, we know that it can be a burden to attend Mass as a family, but even with the best of intentions, a "divide and conquer" mindset toward Mass attendance can unintentionally thwart the family's experience of Mass as a communal event and contribute to a sense in the family that Mass isn't something to prioritize as much as it is something to "get done in the most efficient way possible."

By all means, divide and conquer at the grocery store, with all your errands, with picking up and dropping off kids, and doing your family chores. But when it comes to Mass, barring a major catastrophe, do everything you can to attend Mass as a family.

Volunteer as a family. Earlier, we shared research showing that when kids are given a chance to serve in the name of their faith, they are much more likely to own their faith as adults. When getting involved in parish activities, parish ministries, and parish service projects, we recommend using the same rule of thumb that we employ for other activities — namely, if it's worth doing, it's worth doing as a family.

You've heard of "golf widows" and "football widows" — people whose spouses are so involved in those or other sports that they are virtually absent from the marriage. Well, there are "church widows," "church widowers," and "church orphans" too — wives, husbands, and children who grow to resent the Church because the parish family always seemed to take precedence over family life at home.

Look for opportunities to serve together. If one of you is an altar server or a lector, go to that Mass. If you have a lector, server, and choir member in the family, don't be afraid to ask if you can all serve at the same Mass. Or, when that isn't possible, let the adults or an older child do their service and then return to Mass again later as a family.

Parish picnics, parish schools of religion, youth groups, and other family-oriented parish activities are all great opportunities for families to connect, as a whole, with the wider parish community. Try to favor those ways of interfacing with your parish over more individual ministries and memberships that can pile up and threaten the cohesion of your domestic church.

Be hospitable. Catholics arguably are *terrible* at authentic parish hospitality. Although we don't have anything more than anecdotal evidence to support this, our experience appears to be almost universal. Sure, we have greeters at the doors and occasionally the kiss of peace devolves into a social free-for-all, but that's often as far as parish relationships go.

We're all busy, but being authentically hospitable in your parish gives you an opportunity to choose the "better part" (Luke 10:42, NABRE) and build real, grace-filled relationships outside your home. By "authentic hospitality" we mean going beyond the superficial, corporate gestures of parish hospitality and actually caring enough to introduce yourself to the people sitting next to you in the pew, or inviting a family out to brunch with your family, or looking for other opportunities for you to connect with fellow parishioners outside the four walls of your sanctuary or parish hall.

Our Evangelical Protestant brothers and sisters tend to have it all over us Catholics when it comes to caring about the people they worship with. There are a lot of interesting theories for why this is the case, but they all come down to excuses. We hope you will accept our challenge to you to be a leader in building real relationships in your parish by extending invitations to others to get to know you and your family and by accepting invitations that are extended to you, even if you aren't completely sure the people offering the invitation are a "perfect fit" for you.

In an on-demand world, we're used to ordering whatever we want whenever we want it. With so many options to choose from, we can afford to be picky about our entertainment options. Unfortunately, this self-centered mentality often extends to our social relationships as well. As a society, we have become connoisseurs of people. We want only friends who are perfectly compatible with our spiritual or political or liturgical or socio-economic preferences. We accept invitations—by text—only at the last minute, just in case a more interesting invitation doesn't come along in the meantime. Frankly, this sort of behavior should be beneath us. But more than this, when we adopt this attitude toward the people in our parish community, we miss out on wonderful opportunities to connect with other people who are trying their best to encounter God in their everyday lives. We can't do it alone. We need each other.

In an earlier chapter, we shared research by Christian Smith that mapped the pathways young adults take into the Church. Several of those pathways were characterized by close relationships with faithful peers and adults who were not part of their family. Developing relationships with other families in the parish, giving our kids opportunities to interact with other faithful kids, and becoming involved as parent volunteers in the parish school or in youth-group, parish-based, or community-service projects demonstrates that our faith is lived out not only in the home but also in the world.

Make the parish your extended family. Suggest to your pastor that your parish should see itself as the extended family of all the families in the parish. Propose having a monthly movie night with a discussion of the faith elements in the film; or a game night at your parish that begins with adoration and ends with an extended social time when families bring and share their favorite board and card games; or a monthly dinner celebrating parishioners who had birthdays or anniversaries that month and a Mass during which those parishioners can receive a special blessing. Let your creativity soar as you brainstorm ways to combine fun and faith in a family-friendly way in your parish. In a world where extended families are often separated by hundreds or thousands of miles, our parishes should be stepping into the void to be the extended family of faith.

The Good News!

Parents and families often feel overwhelmed at the thought of living and passing on the faith to our kids. The good news is that we don't have to do it alone. Although parish life, and Catholic school, and parish activities can't substitute for living your faith in your home, these things can be a tremendous help to families by giving you a community of faithful people to support you and offer you godly avenues to carry your faith into the world. Cultivate a family-centered, dynamic, and hospitable attitude toward parish life, and enjoy the infusion of grace you will receive from the Holy Spirit as you connect your family to the extended Family of God.

16

Discovering God Together — for Life

Throughout this book, we have attempted to present the most current research and much practical wisdom about ways you and your
children can discover God together as he resides in your hearts,
your home, your parish community, and your community at large.
That said, no book on this topic could ever hope to address every
possibility. We hope that you will use these ideas as a springboard
for your own creativity and a conduit for the Holy Spirit to set
your hearts ablaze with new ideas for how you can become the
family you were created to be and help each other get to heaven.

As you've come to see throughout this book, passing on the
faith to your kids is not just handing them a box filled with stuff
you inherited from your parents, in the hopes that they will give
the same box filled with the same stuff to their kids, but a lifelong
project of learning and growing together in what it means to be
children of God. There is a saying that "education is not so much
the filling of a bucket as it is the lighting of a fire." It would be
safe to say that this is exponentially truer of faith education,
which involves cooperating with the grace of God's Holy Spirit
to enkindle in our children the fire of God's love!

From God's point of view, you are not only parents to your
children; you are also their older brother and sister in the Lord,

and God asks all of you—all *his* children—to learn more about how to receive and share his love every day. By committing to the ideas in this book and the ideas they inspire, you are setting out on your own spiritual journey; a journey toward greater transformation, greater joy, more authentic love, and deeper intimacy.

Intimacy Drives Discipleship

If we could leave you with just one thing, we would like it to be this idea: that passing the faith on to your children is about seeking always to live a more intimate family life, an intimacy that mirrors—as much as human beings can—the intimacy that exists between the Father, the Son, and the Holy Spirit. Does it sound crazy to say that? Too idealistic? In truth, although it might be surprising to some, Catholics believe that the family is an "icon of the Trinity." In the words of Pope Benedict XVI:

> God is Trinity. He is communion of love, and the family—with all the difference that exists between the Mystery of God and His human creature—is an expression thereof which reflects the unfathomable mystery of God-Love.... The human family is, in a certain sense, the icon of the Trinity because of the love between its members and the fruitfulness of that love. (Angelus, December 27, 2009).

From the Catholic point of view, family life is the closest opportunity we have, this side of heaven, to experience the generous, joyful, loving, mutually self-giving, intimate relationship between the Father, the Son, and the Holy Spirit. Catholic families can't get a more awesome set of marching orders than to hear the Church saying, "You see how the Father, Son, and Holy Spirit relate to each other? Okay. Go create that with your kids."

Our intention in saying this is not to intimidate you. We are all fallen. We all struggle. Families may be icons of the Trinity, but all of us are covered with some degree of residue, mold, dirt, and dross that the heavenly Artist must scrape away before we can do our job of fully revealing God's love. Rather, our hope is to inspire you to strive for the greatness to which you and your family are called.

In *Familiaris Consortio*, Pope St. John Paul the Great wrote:

> The family finds in the plan of God the Creator and Redeemer not only its identity, what it is, but also its mission, what it can and should do. The role that God calls the family to perform in history derives from what the family is; its role represents the dynamic and existential development of what it is. Each family finds within itself a summons that cannot be ignored, and that specifies both its dignity and its responsibility: *family, become what you are.* (no. 17, emphasis ours)

In this inspiring note, St. John Paul II tells families that we are the clearest and most tangible sign of God's love and call to intimate union in the world, and then he tells us to "become what you are."

We cannot hope to pass the faith on to our children unless we are constantly striving, as a family, to do a better job of cultivating the kind of intimacy the Father, Son, and Holy Spirit share.

In his book *The Seven Levels of Intimacy*, Matthew Kelly argues that all relationships have a certain degree of intimacy.

Level 1 is *cliches*, those polite expressions that let others know that we're basically well socialized. "How are you?" "I'm okay." "And how was school?" "It was good." "What did you do today?" "Not much. You?"

Level 2 is *facts*, where we share current events and the stuff of our day with each other. "Nice weather we're having." "I went to the store today." "John got a new video game."

Level 3 is *opinions*, the first level where we pull back a little bit of the curtain on our true selves and at least offer hints at our priorities, values, and ideals. "I didn't think it was very nice for Allison to say that to Marcus." "I think the president is doing a good job."

Level 4 is *hopes and dreams*, where we discuss the kind of people we would like to become someday, our aspirations and goals, our desires and ambitions. "I would really like to own my own business someday." "I would like people to think of me as a faithful and loving person."

Level 5 is *feelings*, where we willingly share the impact that our lives have on us and the impact we have on each other and reflect together on the meaning of it all. "I just feel so close to God when we do that." "I feel so conflicted inside about making this decision."

Level 6 is *fears, faults, and failures*, where we confide in each other about our struggles and get support and encouragement to do better. "I wish I could get a better handle on my temper." "I'm just so worn out by the whole thing. I wish I could be friendlier, but he just irritates me so much!"

Level 7 is *needs*, where we openly share the things we need in life and from each other to feel fulfilled and whole. "I really need you to make some time for us to be together. I'm feeling really disconnected lately."

We share this because, in our experience, too many families don't make it much past level 3, opinions, but a true parent-child discipleship relationship can't happen unless all seven levels are present in family life. That's why we spent so much time discussing the need to reclaim family rituals, practice gentle discipline, and foster attachment and family warmth in a book on faith development. These are the things that will open your children's hearts and allow you to form them in the faith. By and large, it is our observation that many intentional Catholic parents are reasonably good at modeling the faith and at teaching faith concepts to their children, but where even they fall down is in the area of discipleship. People believe that faith should be caught not taught, and, to some degree, that's true. But what is even truer is that lasting, meaningful faith must be formed in an intimate discipleship relationship that not only models faithful behavior and teaches faithful truths but also forms faithful mindsets, worldviews, and ways of relating. And *that's* what this discipleship model we are proposing in *Discovering God Together* excels at.

The more you work to make and maintain the connections that foster a true discipleship relationship between you and your kids, the more likely all the lessons you wish to pass on to your children will stick, and the more authentic your child's encounter with prayer will be. Your children simply cannot have an intimate encounter with a God they cannot see if they don't know how to create intimacy with the people they can experience through all their senses.

Again, no family is perfect and the good news is that you don't need to be. But you do need a vision, and you do need the humility and commitment it takes to try to live that vision in the day-to-day life of your family so that even in your particular brokenness and struggles, the love of God can shine through.

Catholic Families: See How They Love One Another

Many families think it is somehow selfish to work on the quality of their family relationships, or to say no to other activities just so they can have adequate time to be together, but nothing could be further from the truth. As the "school of love and virtue," family life is the most important activity we can commit ourselves to, because in doing so, we polish the icon that reveals the face of God to each other and to the world.

So, in the end, discovering God together and raising faithful children comes down to two simple things: (1) creating an intimate family life that is rooted in the love that comes from God's heart and (2) inviting God to be an intimate part of the daily life of your family so that he can teach you how to master the art of living that love. When families use their creativity and commitment to cooperate with the grace of God and make these two things happen, their homes become more than just a shelter from the storm. They become a beachhead from which God launches his loving counteroffensive against a world consumed by darkness. By becoming what you are, the bright face of God's love in the world, you can encounter all the blessings God wants to share with you and become a positive force for change.

Tertullian once said, "The world says, 'Look at those Christians. See how they love one another.'" We hope you will take up this call and live the kind of godly, grace-filled family life that will allow your children to be inspired by the love they encounter in your faithful home and allow the world to be drawn to the love of Christ shining out of all the windows of your house.

Whom Will You Serve? An Invitation

As Elizabeth Scalia notes in her book *Strange Gods*, we do not live in an age when pagan cults openly worship gold and bronze idols, but we nevertheless live in a world of many gods. Money, sex, coolness, control, technology, our own selves, and other modern objects of worship compete for our attention in the modern spiritual marketplace. Many families have been sacrificed—or have sacrificed themselves—on the altars of these strange gods. Even many Catholic families have forgotten who we really are and who we are truly called to be.

The book of Joshua tells the story of how the people of Israel forgot who they were. For several generations, they had forgotten their identity as God's Chosen People. They neglected their mission. They worshipped other gods. In the face of this, Joshua called his people together. He reminded them of who they were, where they had come from, whose people they were, and to what they were called, and he asked them to make a decision about whom they would serve.

In this modern age of strange gods, a time where family life is devalued and even, at times, derided, a time in which many Catholics have lost their identity and sense of mission, we would suggest that our Catholic families are having our own "Joshua moment." God wants to use our families to change the world, to be his face in the world, to call all people home to him by our example of love, faithfulness, and joy.

You are responding to that call. We applaud your courage in taking up the challenge to be a faithful witness in the world and to join your voice with Joshua's in proclaiming that although other families may live as they choose, "As for me and my house, we will serve the LORD" (Josh. 24:15).

An Invitation from the Authors

Dear Reader,

Throughout this book we have attempted to offer you many suggestions for making your faith come alive both for yourself and your children.

We appreciate, however, that sometimes this can be a difficult road to walk. At times, our own struggles or challenges within our marriage or family life can make living our faith difficult, if not almost impossible. In those times, we would like to offer our support.

Each year, the Pastoral Solutions Institute provides over ten thousand hours of ongoing pastoral psychotherapy services by telephone to Catholic individuals, couples, and families around the world. Through our books, our daily radio program, and our counseling service, we strive to help Catholics live more faithful, grace-filled lives in response to the challenges they face. Our team of counseling professionals are experienced, licensed clinicians who have the benefit of additional training in Catholic theology so you can be sure that the advice and counsel we offer will be supportive of your faith journey.

If we can be of assistance to you or to those you love as you continue to do your best to live the Catholic difference in all you do, we hope that you will call on us. To learn more about ways the Pastoral Solutions Institute can be of service to you, please visit us online at www.CatholicCounselors.com or call to make an appointment at 740-266-6461.

May God bless you abundantly.

Yours in Christ,
Dr. Greg and Lisa Popcak

Appendix

The Spirituality of the Catholic Family in the 21st Century

How do contemporary Catholic families in the United States worship, pray, and learn about God? Following are some high-lights from the CARA study commissioned by Holy Cross Family Ministries and conducted by Mark Gray. For the full study, visit Holy Cross Family Ministries at HCFM.org.

Mass Attendance

- 22 percent of Catholic families attend Mass weekly. Of this group, parents with larger families (three or more children) are more likely (66 percent) to be weekly Mass attendees.

- 31 percent of Catholic families attend Mass at least once a month.

- 15 percent of either separated or divorced parents or never-married parents attend Mass weekly.

- 47 percent of Catholic families attend Mass only "a few times a year or less."

Parents with a teen in the home are more likely to attend Mass weekly (26 percent) than those with an infant (18 percent).

Catholic Education

The following percentages of Catholic families have children enrolled in …

a Catholic elementary or middle school: 8 percent

a Catholic high school: 3 percent

a parish-based Catholic religious education
program (e.g., CCD or parish school):   21 percent

a youth ministry program: 5 percent

Sixty-eight percent of Catholic parents do not have children enrolled in any type of formal faith education.

When faith education is considered in light of Mass attendance, 42 percent of weekly Mass attendees having a child enrolled in a parish-based religious education (although *not* a Catholic school) compared with 27 percent of monthly attendees, 11 percent of those who attend a few times a year, and only 4 percent of those who rarely or never attend Mass.

Likewise the cost of Catholic education does not appear to be the most significant deciding factor in whether to enroll children in Catholic schools. For instance, among those in households earning $85,000 or more per year, only 14 percent have a child enrolled in a Catholic elementary school and 4 percent in a Catholic high school.

Prayer

Apart from Mass attendance:

• 36 percent of Catholic parents pray at least once a day.

• 23 percent pray less often than daily but at least once a week.

The Spirituality of the Catholic Family

- 20 percent pray less often than weekly but at least once a month.

- 12 percent pray a few times a year. Only 9 percent say they rarely or never pray.

Of those Catholic parents who pray:

- 76 percent say that they pray on their own but ...

- 17 percent say that they pray *both* alone *and* together as a family.

- 7 percent say they tend not to pray on their own but do pray with their family in some way.

When Do Catholic Parents Pray?

Prayer at family gatherings is less common than prayer in other settings and at other times. In descending order, parents are most likely "always" to pray:

- during times of crisis (42 percent)

- when feeling anxious or depressed (34 percent)

- when feeling blessed (31 percent)

- before bed (26 percent)

- during Lent (18 percent)

- during Advent (18 percent)

- when they wake (13 percent)

- before meals (13 percent)

- at family gatherings (10 percent)

Here is the breakdown of when Catholic parents say they pray:

	Always	Most of the time	Some of the time	Rarely	Never
During times of crisis	42	25	23	7	3
When I feel anxious or depressed	34	25	26	10	5
When I feel blessed	31	23	26	13	7
Before bed	26	26	25	15	8
During Lent	18	21	28	19	14
During Advent	18	18	26	20	18
When I awake	13	13	29	25	20
Before meals	13	13	25	29	20
At family gatherings	10	13	29	27	21

Why Don't Catholic Families Pray Together?

Of those parents who pray alone, but not with their families, the primary reasons given are as follows: 24 percent simply prefer to pray alone; 21 percent say that schedules do not permit family prayer. In the words of respondents, the following are some reasons why Catholic parents prefer to pray alone rather than with their families:

- Because I like to do it alone. It makes me feel like I can be more open and honest and closer to God.

- My prayers seem like intimate conversations.

The Spirituality of the Catholic Family

- Prayers are said when most of the children are asleep.

- Kids weren't baptized.

- Husband is atheist.

- [When I was] a child, my family only prayed at holiday meals, which is when we do as a family.

- Kids are too little.

When Catholic Parents Pray, How Do They Pray?

	Always	Most of the time	Some of the time	Rarely	Never
Praying for the well-being of your family	52	31	14	2	1
Saying a specific Catholic prayer (e.g., Our Father, Hail Mary)	37	20	22	12	9
Praying for the well-being of others you know (nonfamily)	31	27	31	9	2
Simply talking to God	26	25	31	11	7
Praying for your own well-being	24	21	39	13	4
Praying for world issues (e.g., peace, to relieve human suffering)	21	20	32	19	8
Reflecting on something	13	19	44	14	10
Meditating	11	11	31	25	22
Discerning something	10	10	36	26	18
Participating in other religious devotions	8	7	28	28	29

Recommended Resources

Faithful Parenting/Discipling Your Children

Parenting with Grace: The Catholic Parents' Guide to Raising (Almost) Perfect Kids, by Dr. Gregory K. and Lisa Popcak

Then Comes Baby: The Catholic Guide to Surviving and Thriving in the First Three Years of Parenthood, by Dr. Gregory K. and Lisa Popcak

Six Sacred Rules for Families: A Spirituality for the Home, by Tim and Sue Muldoon

A Catholic Parents' Tool Box: Raising Healthy Families in the 21st Century, by Dr. Joseph D. White

Forming Intentional Disciples: The Path to Knowing and Following Jesus, by Sherry Weddell

Raising Moral Kids

Beyond the Birds and the Bees: Raising Sexually Whole and Holy Children, by Dr. Gregory K. and Lisa Popcak

Neurobiology and the Development of Human Morality: Evolution, Culture, and Wisdom, by Darcia Narvaez

Discovering God Together

Catholic Traditions and Prayer

The Catholic Home, by Meredith Gould

The Big Book of Catholic Customs and Traditions, by Anne Neuberger

Catholic Household Blessings and Prayers, by the U.S. Conference of Catholic Bishops

Your Life in the Spirit: What Every Catholic Needs to Know and Experience, by Alan Schreck

Sober Intoxication of the Spirit (parts 1 and 2), by Fr. Raniero Cantalamessa

How to get more out of the Rosary: FamilyRosary.org

Explaining and Defending the Faith

Friendly Defenders Cards, by Matt Pinto

Prove It! series (God, Faith, Church, Jesus, You), by Amy Welborn

Did Adam and Eve Have Belly Buttons?: And 199 Other Questions from Catholic Teenagers, by Matt Pinto

Ask the Bible Geek: Answers to Questions from Catholic Teens, by Mark Hart

References

Ainsworth, M. D. S., and S. M. Bell (1970). "Attachment, Exploration, and Separation: Illustrated by the Behavior of One-Year-Olds in a Strange Situation." *Child Development* 41:49–67.

Bengtson, V. (2013). *Families and Faith: How Religion Is Passed Down across Generations.* Oxford University Press.

Beck, R., and A. McDonald (2004). "Attachment to God: The Attachment to God Inventory, Tests of Working Model Correspondence, and an Exploration of Faith Group Differences." *Journal of Psychology and Theology* 32:92–103.

Catechism of the Catholic Church (1995). U.S. Catholic Conference—Libreria Editrice Vaticana.

Craven, M. (2011). "Fathers: Key to Their Children's Faith." *Christian Post*, June 19, 2011. Retrieved April 6, 2015. http://www.christianpost.com/news/fathers-key-to-their-childrens- faith-51331/.

Fiese, B. (2006). *Family Routines and Rituals.* New Haven, CT: Yale University Press.

Fowler, J. (1995). *Stages of Faith: The Psychology of Human Development and the Quest for Meaning.* New York: Harper One.

Gray, M., and T. Gaunt (2015). *Faith in the Family: A Survey of U.S. Catholic Parents for Holy Cross Family Ministries* by the Center for Applied Research in the Apostolate.

Haug, W., and P. Warner (2000). *The Demographic Characteristics of National Minorities in Certain European States,* vol. 2. *Population Studies,* no. 31.

John Paul II (1995). *Evangelium Vitae.*http://w2.vatican.va/content/john-paul-ii/en/encyclicals/documents/hf_jp-ii_enc_25031995_evangelium-vitae.html.

John Paul II (2006). *Man and Woman He Created Them: A Theology of the Body.* Translated by Michael Waldstein. Boston: Pauline Books and Media.

Marquardt, E. (2006). *Between Two Worlds: The Inner Lives of Children of Divorce.* New York: Harmony.

Marquardt, E. (2011). "The Spirituality of Children of Divorce." *Huffington Post: The Blog.* Retrieved May 4, 2015. http://www.huffingtonpost.com/elizabeth-marquardt/the-spirituality-of-child_b_798400.html

Neufeld, G., and G. Maté (2006). *Hold On to Your Kids. Why Parents Need to Matter More Than Peers.* New York: Ballantine Books.

Nordhagen, L. (2001). *When Only One Converts.* Huntington, IN: Our Sunday Visitor.

Oliner, S., and P. Oliner (1992). *The Altruistic Personality: Rescuers of the Jews in Nazi Europe.* New York: Touchstone.

References

Pargament, K. (2011). *Spiritually Integrated Psychotherapy. Understanding and Addressing the Sacred.* New York: Guilford Press.

Paul VI (1974). *Marialis Cultus.* http://w2.vatican.va/content/paul-vi/en/apost_exhortations/documents/hf_p-vi_exh_19740202_marialis-cultus.html.

Popcak, G., and L. Popcak (2010). *Parenting with Grace: The Catholic Parents' Guide to Raising (Almost) Perfect Kids.* Huntington, IN: Our Sunday Visitor.

Popcak, G., and L. Popcak (2014). *Then Comes Baby: The Catholic Guide to Surviving and Thriving in the First Three Years of Parenthood.* Notre Dame, IN: Ave Maria Press.

"Pope Benedict XVI on the Family, an 'Icon of the Trinity' and 'the Best School.'" *Ignatius Insight Scoop.* December 28, 2009. Retrieved May 4, 2015. http://insightscoop.typepad.com/2004/2009/12/pope-benedict-xvi-on-the-family-an-icon-of-the-trinity-and-the-best-school.html.

Smith, C., K. Longest, and J. Hill (2014). *Young Catholic America: Emerging Adults, In, Out of, and Gone from the Church.* New York: Oxford University Press.

Sunderland, M. (2008). *The Science of Parenting.* New York: DK.

Weddell, S. (2012). *Forming Intentional Disciples: The Path to Knowing and Following Jesus.* Huntington: IN: Our Sunday Visitor.

Weddell, S. Personal communication. March 26, 2015.

About the Authors

Gregory K. and Lisa Popcak

Dr. Greg and Lisa Popcak are the founders and directors of the Pastoral Solutions Institute and hosts of More2Life Radio. Together, they have authored almost twenty books and programs. For more information on their tele-counseling practice and other resources, visit www.CatholicCounselors.com.

* * *

Other Books and Programs
by Greogry K. and Lisa Popcak

MARRIAGE AND SEXUALITY

Just Married
The Catholic Guide to Surviving and
Thriving in the First Five Years of Marriage

Holy Sex!
The Catholic Guide to Toe-Curling,
Mind-Blowing, Infallible Loving

For Better . . . FOREVER!
A Catholic Guide to Lifelong Marriage

The Exceptional Seven Percent
Nine Secrets of the World's Happiest Couples

When Divorce Is Not an Option
How to Heal Your Marriage
and Nurture Lasting Love

PARENTING AND FAMILY

Then Comes Baby
The Catholic Guide to Surviving and Thriving
in the First Three Years of Parenthood

Beyond the Birds and the Bees
Raising Sexually Whole and Holy Kids

Parenting with Grace
The Catholic Parents' Guide to
Raising (Almost) Perfect Kids

FAITH AND LIFE

God Help Me,
These People Are Driving Me Nuts!
Making Peace with Difficult People

God Help Me,
This Stress Is Driving Me Crazy!
Finding Balance Through God's Grace

The Life God Wants You to Have
Discovering the Divine Plan When Human Plans Fail

An Invitation

Reader, the book that you hold in your hands was published by Sophia Institute Press. Sophia Institute seeks to nurture the spiritual, moral, and cultural life of souls and to spread the Gospel of Christ in conformity with the authentic teachings of the Roman Catholic Church.

Our press fulfills this mission by offering translations, reprints, and new publications that afford readers a rich source of the enduring wisdom of mankind.

We also operate two popular online Catholic resources: CrisisMagazine.com and CatholicExchange.com.

Crisis Magazine provides insightful cultural analysis that arms readers with the arguments necessary for navigating the ideological and theological minefields of the day. *Catholic Exchange* provides world news from a Catholic perspective as well as daily devotionals and articles that will help you to grow in holiness and live a life consistent with the teachings of the Church.

In 2013, Sophia Institute launched Sophia Institute for Teachers to renew and rebuild Catholic culture through service to Catholic education. With the goal of nurturing the spiritual, moral, and cultural life of souls, and an abiding respect for the role and work of teachers, we strive to provide materials and programs that are at once enlightening to the mind and ennobling to the heart; faithful and complete, as well as useful and practical.

www.SophiaInstitute.com
www.CatholicExchange.com
www.CrisisMagazine.com
www.SophiaInstituteforTeachers.org

Sophia Institute Press® is a registered trademark of Sophia Institute. Sophia Institute is a tax-exempt institution as defined by the Internal Revenue Code, Section 501(c)(3). Tax I.D. 22-2548708.